THE
DECORATIVE ART
OF
RUSSIA

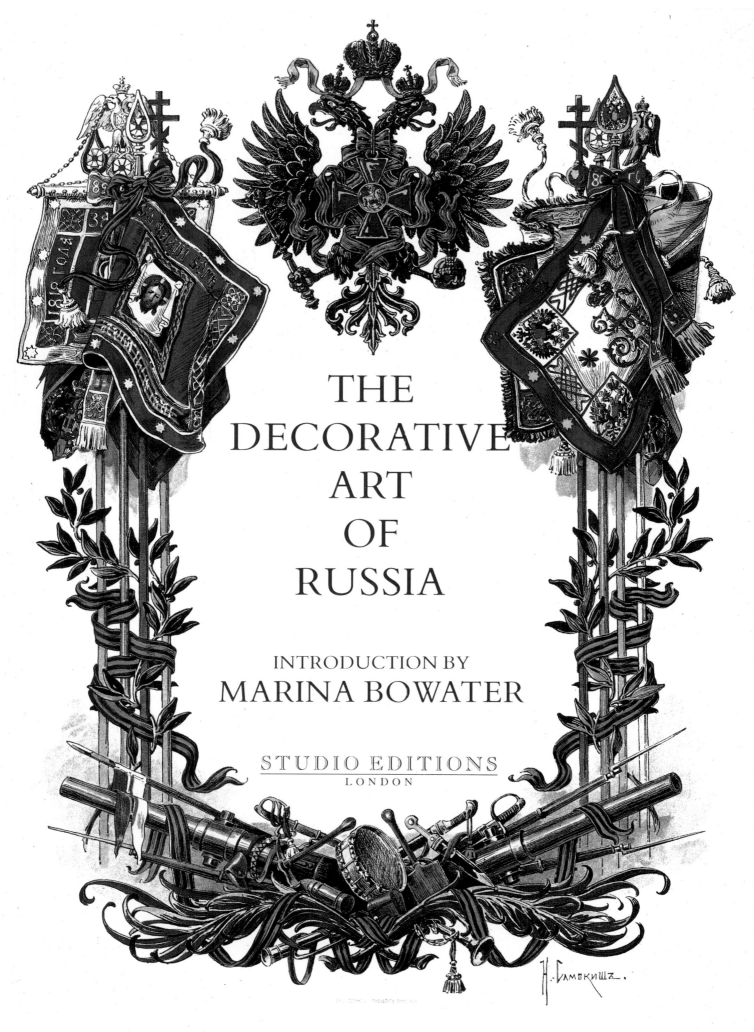

THE DECORATIVE ART OF RUSSIA

INTRODUCTION BY
MARINA BOWATER

STUDIO EDITIONS
LONDON

TO PRINCE AND PRINCESS NIKITA ROMANOV

Published by Studio Editions Ltd.
Princess House, 50 Eastcastle Street
London W1N 7AP
ENGLAND

The Decorative Art of Russia
was previously published in 1887
under the title
Slavonic and Eastern Ornamentation
with the authority of
his Majesty Emperor Alexander II

and contains a selection of colour transparencies courtesy of
Christies, Sothebys, The Winter Palace, Raymond F. Piper Collection and Marina Bowater

ISBN 1 85170 355 1

Printed and bound in Hong Kong

CONTENTS

ACKNOWLEDGEMENTS

I should like to thank the following for their help
and permission to use photographs:
The Raymond F. Piper Collection, Plate 66;
Christie's Colour Library, Plates 61, 67, 68, 69,
70, 72, 74, 75, 76, 77, 78, 79, 80, 82, 83, 84, 85,
86, 88, 89, 91, 92, 95, 97, 99, 100;
Sotheby's, Plates 65, 71, 81, 87, 90, 93, 96, 98;
The Winter Palace, Plates 62, 63, 64, 73.

INTRODUCTION

THE incredible richness, variety and vitality of Russian decorative art and the strongly-established tradition of iconography and pictorial decoration of objects makes it particularly difficult to draw anything other than an arbitrary line between the fine and decorative arts of Russia. I have taken the view that to maintain a rigidly purist stance would not serve our purpose here, which is to illustrate the best of Russian decorative art in all its magnificence; inevitably therefore, there must be some overlap.

The multi-ethnic peoples of that vast land mass we call Russia descend from ancestors of near-eastern and East European origin including the various tribes (Scythians, Sarmatians, Severiani, Polyane and Ilichi). In today's geographical terminology, 'Russia' is strictly the Russian Soviet Federal Socialist Republic, the largest, most densely populated and influential of the Soviet republics, which before the revolution of 1917, constituted the Russian Empire. Long after the arrival of Christianity in the tenth century, slight elements of the old pagan customs continued, so the influences on Russian decorative imagery were manifold.

Eastern European history tended to be even more turbulent than that of the West, and that of the Russian Empire particularly so because of the wild and militant peoples living on its borders. The most aggressive of these were the Tartars and the Mongols – the former being subservient to the latter, and both paying homage to the Great Khan. In the mid-thirteenth century, having conquered Northern China, the Caucasus, Persia and later, Northern India, they moved west and overran Russia and Eastern Europe. They finally withdrew into the steppe-country where they established themselves at Sarai, on the river Volga, and harassed the Russian lands for some three centuries to come if with diminishing effect towards the end of their ascendancy. They came to be known as the *Zolotaia Orda*, or the Golden Horde.

The Horde did not invade the northernmost regions of 'ancient Rus' because their mounted armies could not manoeuvre in such densely forested areas. Nevertheless, they demanded and received heavy tribute, and as a result, Russia, while trying to survive, enjoyed no artistic renaissance. Punitive raids by the Tartars were frequent and numerous slaves were taken; wooden planks were placed across the bound, living bodies of prisoners on which feasting took place; they moved in such numbers that rings of mounted warriors could circle a town or an army for months at a time in relays, their catapults gradually reducing all resistance. The only areas of safety were the monastery-fortresses and fortified churches, to which, paradoxically in view of their ferocity, the khans granted an *erlyk* (a charter) for their protection. And it was in these locations of comparative safety where for many decades the creative arts were fostered. Here it was that the tradition of icon painting grew up, an art form which became the central element of Russian culture.

During the centuries preceding the bringing of Christianity to his vast domains (in 989) by the Great Prince of Kievan Rus, Vladimir *Ravnoapostolny* ('the Equal of Apostles') a title which is given to those people who Christianise a country), numerous peoples inhabited the wide and fertile lands between the Carpathians and the River Don – the rich black-earth country. The most important of these were the sophisticated settled Scythians, and a people of Iranian stock, the nomadic Sarmations. These ceded to one another and their social intercourse saw the emergence of the Slav (the Ante or Rusak), whose lands came to be known as Rus. There were wars and invasions until the tribal principalities and city states merged, and a unified culture emerged which centred on a town standing on the edge of that great waterway, the Dnieper, which served to unite the northern regions with the south, and with the Byzantine Empire. This town was Kiev. And it is from Kievan Rus, 'the cradle of Russian civilization', that 'modern' Russian history unfolded.

The *kurgany* (burial mounds) of these various peoples have revealed surprisingly sophisticated artifacts – zoomorphic and anthropomorphic brooches clasps and other jewellery, golden chains of the most complicated design, bowls and crucibles and other domestic implements, planes, axes, remnants of harness and skates. A magnificent golden comb was discovered at the turn of the twentieth century; various figures of ancient deities, and Greek and Roman coins often make their appearance during archaeological digs (Roman towns and garrisons existed from the regions of present-day Hungary to the Azov).

Not the least important of the ancient deities was the god *Peroun of the Silver Head and the Golden Moustache*, the god of thunder, lightning and just about everything else, to whom people clung with tenacious persistence up to the time of the adoption of Christianity. There were also the goddess of water, *Mokosh*,

8

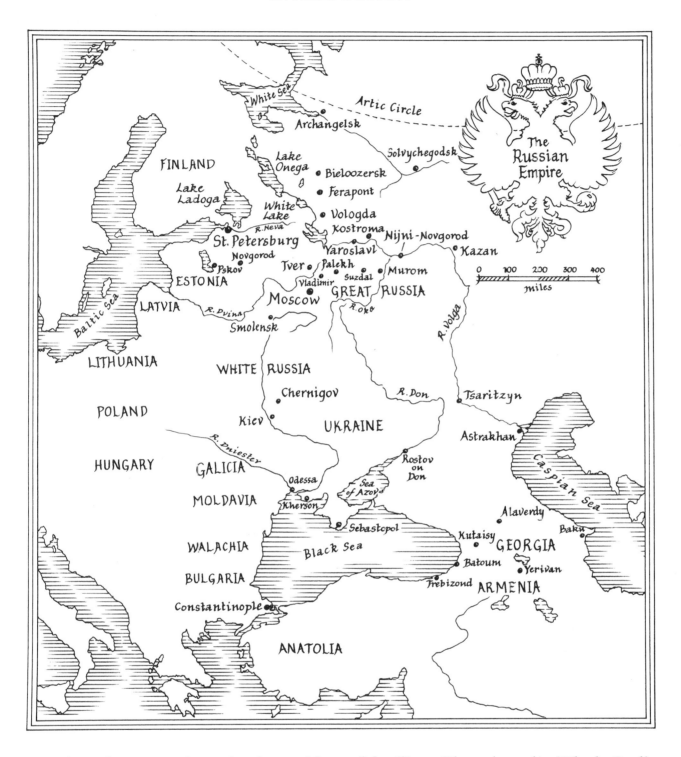

Dazbog, the sun god, *Lada*, the goddess of fertility, *Chernabog*, the 'Black God', and the oldest gods of all – *Rod* and *Rajhanitzy*, the gods of forefathers. The far north harboured *Jumala*, the 'Golden Goddess', and her cult is said to extend into present times. Legend has it that she still exists in the remote taiga-regions of northernmost Siberia and the Urals, and expeditions continue to make probes in search of her vast, hollow golden idol inside which there is another, and another. The idol sings when the wind passes through it. Ancient maps exist on which small gold specks indicate the one-time locations of her presence. The small,

9

highly- coloured 'nest' dolls which unscrew to reveal another and then another are considered to be a disguise for *Jumala*; they were banned by the all-powerful Orthodox Church authorities in medieval times. All these deities, many of whom developed into folk-lore even taking on different identities, served to inspire material of the most diversified nature for the decorative arts of Russia.

In precisely the same manner as in the West, minstrels spread folk tales through the country, and many *basni* and *byliny* (epic poems and heroic tales) have been handed down. One of the best-known of the minstrels was Boyan, who lived in the eleventh century – the 'nightingale of the days of old': when he wished to draw attention to himself, he would release ten falcons at a flight of swans, then, having achieved his aim, he would begin his performance accompanying himself on a *guzly* (psaltery). Such men were the first popular historians before written records. The first Russian learned historian, however, was Nestor the Scribe (a monk at the Kievan Monastery of the Caves), whose book, *The Chronicle of Ancient Years* or *The First Annals*, brings us through to the year 1100. Both Nestor the Scribe and Boyan are mentioned in the twelfth century *Lay of Prince Igor's Regiment*.

The rich resources of Russian folk culture, encompassing as they do, so vast an area, inspired innumerable styles and varieties of decorative artistry, but to trace their origins is no easy matter. A book entitled *Slavianski i Vostochny Ornament* (*Slavonic and Eastern Ornamentation*), collected and researched by Vladimir Vassilievich Stassov (1824–1906), the son of the renowned architect, Vassili Petrovich Stassov, (1769–1848), who was also art critic, historian and music biographer, was among the first to provide a study of his country's history of design, including calligraphy at which the Novgorodian and Stroganov artists excelled, although it is perhaps, the least known and discussed of Russian art forms.

Russian art is easily recognizable despite the influences to which it was subjected through the centuries. Its main characteristics are its vibrant colour, vitality and a tremendous sense of poetry in movement. This is reflected particularly strongly in iconography which was inherited from the Byzantines during the tenth century. The strict and ascetic Greek depictions very quickly assumed their own essentially Russian individuality – the difference in interpretation can be paralleled by the brilliantly clear *plein air* painting of the Impressionists (many of whom used icons as their touchstones), and the muted and more formal work of the Salon artists.

Thus we witness a growing culture, the emergence of political stability and the dominance of the Slav in Eastern Europe which was, naturally, reflected in Slavonic arts. The thirteenth century saw the translation of power from Kiev and Vladimir to Moscow, where its great princes, then tsars, and finally the emperors

(Peter the Great assumed the title in 1712), ruled until the cataclysmic events of 1917: though latterly, of course, they ruled from St Petersburg.

Icon painting often features in Russian ornamentation, but it does not feature in the country's secular painting. Secular painting did not exist in Russia until the second half of the seventeenth century, at which time *parsuna* portraits began to make their appearance. *Parsuna* is a corruption of the Italian word *persona*, and it describes the stiff and stylised manner in which the early portraits were painted. This was so because an icon is a consecrated object of veneration, and any representation of human likeness (whether pictorial or sculptured) for secular purposes was considered by the established Church to be blasphemous. Icons were painted according to strict canonic rules and in a highly stylised manner. Like the Bible and the Gospels, they were the peoples' spiritual textbooks. Any deviation from these established rules for their presentation was forbidden on pain of excommunication, or worse.

In addition to the Christian religious images incorporated into the decorative arts, certain other subjects were particularly popular. The two wondrous half-bird half-woman creatures called *Sirin* and *Alconist*, for example, are very often used decoratively. Their origins are shrouded in the mists of time, but legend has it that they sang so sweetly that they were permitted to live in Paradise. Another, similar creature called *Obida*, with her wings spread wide, represented evil, as did the wolf, *Koshchei the Deathless One* and a witch, *Babba Igga*. Winged horses, lions and griffins, cockerels, peacocks and the *Firebird*, the dot and comma of the Scythians, symmetric and asymmetric patterns, geometrically arranged floral designs, wood nymphs, water sprites (*Russalka*) and forest demons, the Bogatyri (ancient knights of heroic legend), form the central and traditional imagery of ethnic Russian art. Originating in ancient India, the *svastika* found its way to Russia where it became a favoured sign representing good fortune. The Imperial two-headed eagle, too, was very often a prominently displayed decorative feature, more often than not for patriotic reasons. The eagle was adopted for use as a national emblem by Ivan III (1462–1505) when he married the last Byzantine Emperor's niece, Sophia Paléologue, and it remained in use until it was replaced by the hammer and sickle in 1917.

Among the most intriguing and essentially Russian crafts is the working of malachite. Malachite is a stone whose natural shadings range from blueish turquoise, through shades of green to near black, and in section, it has an interesting design which is produced by its sinter formation. It is found in the Ural regions of central Russia but not all its varieties can be processed, for it is liable to powder away under the slightest application of pressure. Its working, which the Russians perfected, particularly after the finding of the Demidov Rock in 1835, is a fascinating subject in itself. The ingenuity of its processing – it was always veneered – incorporated the use of tens of thousands of malachite chips to produce an impression of monumental structures like those of marble, which of course, are cut from vast blocks of limestone in crystalline state. The entire art of working malachite has been in decline for well over a hundred years, and many recipes for fixing masses such as the *Green Crocus* are no longer known. It is said, however, that research work is taking place in the Soviet Union today in an effort to re-create the beauty which once represented an essentially Russian form of artistic production. The Italians, although masters of the lapidary arts, generally produced only small objects in malachite.

Enamelled work in Russia which became a highly developed art form in the nineteenth century, dates from pre-Tartar times. Latter-day jewellers and goldsmiths of the calibre of Ovchinnikov, Morozov, Sazykov and Fabergé had few equals.

Wood-working and carving were, perhaps, the most widespread of the traditional Russian art forms of medieval Russia. Lacking the availability of stone, most churches, palaces and houses were timber built and very little changed until the sixteenth century when vertical boarding came into general use. Until that time, interlocking logs, raised on foundations of boulders, often without the use of a single nail, had been the sole means of construction, and most artifacts were made of treen. A great deal of thought went into the working of wood, and the carvers and carpenters, coopers, cabinet makers and wood turners displayed great imagination.

Sculpture in the round, like secular portraiture, banned by the established church, did not come into existence in Russia until the later seventeenth century, but carving and *bas relief*, often achieving considerable levels of sophistication, had existed from early times. By the eighteenth century the production of carved and decorated furniture, and particularly the Karelian birch variety for example, had reached standards comparable with those of Western Europe. The small stunted Karelian birch tree grows in the tundra wastes of the Karelian peninsula in Russia's extreme north, and is twisted and gnarled, producing interesting patterns in section, with dots in black and brown on a honey-coloured field, various shades of honey, but never brown. It is a wood of great character and individuality little known in the west but which suited the Russian neo-Classical styles to perfection.

Other materials worked by carvers, included walrus tusks, deer antlers, beef bones, tigers' teeth and mammoth tusks from Siberia. There were many centres where 'Russian ivory' and bone were transformed into jewellery, combs, crosses and icons, goblets and caskets or *lartzy*, models of deer teams and dashing troikas, baskets, frames, paper knives – even portraiture: an interesting collection of ivory miniatures carved by Russia's possibly greatest sculptor, the eighteenth-century

Fedot Shubin, represents some sixty rulers of Russian territories from the time of Rurik, the Norse prince who was invited to rule in Russia by the Slavs in 860 AD. Among the better known centres where this work was executed – work which often achieved tracery of filigree fineness – were Kholmogory in the northern region, Tobolsk in Western Siberia, Kislavodsk in the Caucasian foothills, Khotkovo and even Moscow itself. In 1649, Tsar Alexis Mikhailovich (the second Romanov tsar) decreed bonework to be a State monopoly, and carvers were brought from these places to the *Orouzheinaia Palata* – the Armoury Palace's workshops in the Kremlin. In time, due to the pressures of mass production, the art became a craft both imitative and purely repetitive, and the essential naïvité and charm of the earlier work was lost.

Following the interregnum that took place on the death of Ivan the Terrible's son-in-law, Tsar Boris Godunov (in 1605), and the election of Tsar Alexis's father, Mikhail Fedorovich Romanov to the empty throne of all the Russias, stabilisation was the priority for the administrators of Russian government. Although this was accomplished, the country was still backward and riddled with superstition. Foreign mercenaries, marauders and bands of foot-loose Tartars continued to roam about at will. It was not until Tsar Alexis's youngest son, Peter, ascended the throne that Russia's fortunes underwent a metamorphosis.

Peter Romanov was born to Tsar Alexis's second wife in 1672, and on that Tsar's and his eldest son, Fedor III's demise in 1782, a co-tsardom was inaugurated with Peter and his elder half-brother, Ivan V, reigning under the Regency of the Tsarevna Sophia (Ivan's sister) until 1689. In that year the quiet and unenterprising Ivan retired of his own volition and Peter assumed full powers as *Samoderjhavetz* (sole ruler). From that time on, this Tsar's brilliant, if often heavy hand cannot be escaped in any of his country's fields of enterprise.

The story of Russia's development can be said to divide into two distinct periods – the pre- and the post-Petrine eras: the first one having been under the influence of the Byzantine Empire, the second under that of the West. Peter the Great's 'Grand Embassy' of 1697–8 to Western Europe, opened his eyes to his country's backward state, its ignorance of modern techniques and technology, armaments, fashion and various aspects of the arts.

After making a close study of western enterprise, political mechanics and *modus vivendi*, Peter returned home to create constructive havoc among his people. He imported technicians and engineers, gardeners and architects, artists and professors, and set them all to work to bring his country into the eighteenth century. No obstacles were permitted to stand in the way of the Tsar's will.

In 1703 Peter began the building of St Petersburg (today called Leningrad although many residents call it 'Piter'), to which, in 1712, he moved his seat of government from Moscow. This provided his greatly needed 'Window on the

West', and a perfectly positioned relatively ice-free port on the Baltic. (St Petersburg's hegemony, however, was not destined to last for long: 1917 saw the new Soviet authorities return the seat of government to Moscow.

Peter the Great was a rough-and-ready man, uncouth, ruthless and a typical soldier of his day. He had little time for art, but, realising its worth and necessity to the cultural development of his country, he closed down the Kremlin's Armoury Palace workshops and brought most of his artists to his new capital city. Some of these, whom he called his 'fledglings', he sent off to various western capital cities to learn the secrets of their artistic and other achievements. Others he lodged at the Printing House, which was sometimes mistakenly called 'the Academy of Arts', but which was in fact simply an adjunct of St Petersburg's Office of Works, to which he also brought some of his foreign tutors. Although initially it was a school of drawing, it was from there that the Russian artists began their journeys on what must have been an extremely difficult road along which they were expected to rid themselves of drawing and painting iconographically (i.e. according to the restrictive, stylised Church canon), in tempera and on prepared panels, and to transfer to painting in oils on stretched canvas, incorporating the third dimension and, thereby, realism.

In spite of Peter's magnificent foresight, enterprise and imagination, he was directly responsible for the deterioration in quality of iconographic production. Realism, which Tsar Alexis and his fundamentalist Patriarch of Russia, Nicon, had fought so valiantly to contain, finally killed the greatness of Russia's superb and traditional school of iconography.

The Russian eighteenth century was dominated by a succession of formidable women rulers: the four men's reigns lasted for nine collective years and are barely worth a mention. It was with the accession of Elizabeth Petrovna that Russia can be said to have entered a veritable 'Russian Renaissance', with matters moving with considerable speed, the groundwork for their progress having been laid by her father. Her more important predecessor, the Empress Anna Ioanovna (Peter's niece), had not been laggardly in her promotion of the arts, but she had been lax in seeing to maintenance and Elizabeth inherited many problems.

Buildings, bridges and churches were crumbling away due to the rigours of Russia's extreme climatic changes and other factors, and all these things the new Empress took in hand, put right and maintained. She also built extravagantly, ably assisted by her favourite architect, the great exponent of 'Russian Baroque', Count Bartolomeo Rastrelli, so that in the end, St Petersburg came to be surrounded by palaces as Moscow was by monastery-fortresses.

But Elizabeth was no fool, and the people with whom she associated were erudite and progressive. These included her lovers one of whom, Count Ivan Shuvalov, was the first Director of the Academy of Arts. Following in her father's footsteps she promoted all the arts, and she brought into being the Imperial Porcelain Factory. Its story is, possibly, among the most exciting ones that are connected with the arts of Russia.

Following a great many fruitless attempts to glean the secret of porcelain making from China, Western Europe found the formula through its own efforts: the breakthrough was in Saxony in 1708. the Russians, however, continued trying to purchase the formula from China, but none of the transactions that took place involving large sums of money produced satisfactory results. The Chinese language in which the 'formula' was set out proved untranslatable. Accordingly, orders went out and funds were made available for its creation. Certain foreigners were hired for the project, but they all failed to live up to their claims to knowledge, and it fell to a young Russian scientist from Suzdal, Dmitri Vinogradov (1720–59), who had been engaged by the nascent factory's administrator, Baron Tcherkassov, to be discoverer of Russia's own true porcelain, in 1751. (A certain small town near Moscow called Gzhel, a centre of the ceramic industry, claims to have discovered the elusive formula even earlier. A claim which Tcherkassov is said to have dismissed as fantasy. Yet porcelain is known to have been produced there later in the century, but of an inferior quality.)

Initially and understandably, output at the Imperial Factory consisted of small and insignificant objects – bowls, cups and saucers, dishes, jugs – but gradually greater variety entered production – hinged boxes, chocolate cups and covers, coffee and tea pots, baskets with delicately pierced borders, Gospel covers: it was not long before full and spectacular dinner services *surtout de table*, tazzas and vases were able to compete with the best that Saxe or Sèvres had to offer.

Small figurines, or *kouklaki*, too, became a sought after item of production. A modeller called Jean Rachette launched his first series of figurines of ethnic peoples of the Empire in 1779 – Mongols, Cossacks, Kulmaks, Eskimoes and Lapps, all of which enjoyed immediate success as did his miniatures of Russians – *the cobbler, the coachman, the spinner, the three drunks, the milkmaid, the girl with a broken pitcher*, and the others: a group called *the boar hunt* was the earliest recorded product.

As the Imperial Factory grew and expanded (it is now called the State Porcelain Factory), others came into being, several of them rivalling it in the quality of their production, if not in quantity. Among the more important were the Gardner and Popov manufactories, the Postygin, Fomin, Batenin and Terekov, the Kisselov-Sapiegin, the Miklashevsky and the two later giants, the Korniov and the Kuznetzov factories. In 1896 the Kuznetzov factory bought out the historic Gardner Factory: permission was applied for and granted for the Gardner trademark to be retained.

The manufacture of porcelain, glass, *paper mâché*, treen and metal Easter eggs became fashionable in the nineteenth century, although the tradition of presenting eggs (usually hens' eggs painted red) at Easter-time dates from the earliest of Christian times in Russia. Their decoration was always religious, with icons of Christ, the Mother of God (as the Virgin Mary is called in Russia), and the various saints being traditional. Later in the nineteenth century their decoration included stylised designs or flowers, and the Imperial family developed the habit of having their crowned cyphers painted on eggs for presentation as gifts – the quality of an egg being in keeping with the importance of the occasion. Small, white eggs carrying the various Imperial cyphers on one side, and a small red cross on the other, were manufactured during the First World War for presentation to the troops, the nursing services (my mother received one such egg from the Empress personally), and to industrial workers. The red cross serves to date eggs made between the years 1914–17.

A delightful custom came into being for miniature *brelki* in the form of eggs to be given as Easter gifts: infants were presented with these, and by the time they were adults they were in possession of enough to form marvellous necklaces. Carl Fabergé, one of the favoured court jewellers, made his name when he invented the *objet de vitrine* eggs. These, which delighted the sad and harassed Nicholas and Alexandra, found their way to the West at the time of the Revolution and are now much sought by collectors.

Knowledge of glass-making, enamelling and mosaic had existed in pre-Christian Kiev, but for several centuries most knowledge of artistic production is confused and contradictory. It was not until the sixteenth century that reliable information began to re-appear. By this time, the Tartars had finally been routed, and record keeping, stabilisation and order had entered into Russian life. In 1637, for example, a Swede named Elias Koët set up a glass manufactory at Mojhaisk, and another near Moscow. State owned glassworks were operational at Izmailovsk and in the Sparrow Hills, but they closed down in 1713 to be re-opened under private ownership. Window glass was produced at Vladimir, also near Moscow, dating from 1725. Two private proprietors of glassworks were, A. Minter and V. Malzev, who operated ambitious projects at Dmitrov and Moscow: one of their factories still continues in operation, is known as the *Guz-Khroustalny Zavod*, and is the centre of glassmaking in the Soviet Union today. Further documentation proves that the Crown owned other works at Yamburg and Jhabino, and that the eighteenth century saw the Ust-Ruditskaya and Shlisselberg factories come into being.

The Imperial Glassworks in St Petersburg was inaugurated during the reign of the Empress Elizabeth and although glass was seldom signed, the letters M.K. ('P.K.'), meaning Crown Office, can sometimes be found scratched upon the bases of articles. Such pieces are often decorated with crowned Imperial cyphers, with each monarch's personal cypher producing clear identification of the reign during which the piece was made in much the same manner as in the case of porcelain.

The development of the glass industry in Russia was greatly influenced by a man of unique abilities, Mikhail Vassilievich Lomonossov (1711–1775), who like the sculptor, Fedot Ivanovich Shubin, came from the Kholmogory area by the White Sea, and was the son of a well-to-do, free peasant family. As Shubin was sent to study in St Petersburg, Lomonossov went to Moscow: in 1730 he entered the Slavonic-Greco-Latin Academy where he acquired a fluency in Latin: he studied philosophy, then went on to travel and to complete his tuition at Marburg, in Germany. On his return to Russia he was appointed to the Academy of Sciences. The extraordinary range of interests that were encompassed by this man, all of which he investigated and perfected by practical and thorough application, very soon led to his acquiring an international reputation for his genius. He wrote extensively, and, perhaps surprisingly in view of his early background, his prose and poetry were of so high a standard that he is regarded as having changed the Russian language. He set a formidable goal for the oncoming coterie of nineteenth-century writers to live up to – Pushkin, Krylov and Tioutchev, Lermontov, Dostoievsky, Chekhov and Tolstoy among others. In his spare time he indulged in the second of his main interests, mosaic.

In 1751 the Ministry for the Interior requested the Academy of Sciences to loan Lomonossov to the Imperial Glassworks to help them perfect the technique of producing coloured glass. He was seconded to the factory's laboratory where he proceeded to instruct, and to develop his inventions. In time Lomonossov was obliged to return to the Academy, but he was dissatisfied with this arrangement, there still remained certain hues necessary for his experiments. He requested and received a plot of land not far from St Petersburg on which he built a small factory. He named it Ust Rudinskaya, and production commenced in 1754. Now he was able to conduct all the experiments that were necessary to his research. He also spent time on his work on mosaic. He concentrated on portraiture, topography, but not on iconography. He was responsible for the monumental picture of the *Battle of Poltave*, which is fifteen feet high and twenty feet long, and it took him four years to complete. Another huge mosaic, the *Surrender of Azov*, remains unfinished.

In his work Lomonossov used the larger pieces of tesserae, preferring them to the smaller ones which the Italians favoured. His colours were less delicate than those of the Italians, but his work was inventive and many novel techniques were entered into. Lomonossov's studio on the Moica Canal in St Petersburg did not survive him for long, for mosaic as an art form was not popular in Russia other than for table and floor decoration. He once laid down a mosaic floor himself in the Chinese Palace's Glass Study at Oranienbaum (today's Lomonossov), but it did not survive the years. Some of his table tops, which were a combination of glass tesserae and marble, have, fortunately, been preserved.

During the late eighteenth century the Imperial Glassworks began to produce cut and facetted glass of high quality. Massive chandeliers and candelabra made their appearance, and these were often married to malachite and other minerals, as well as to fire-gilt bronze 'in the Russian style', and with dazzling effect. Such marriages were greatly favoured, and objects of clear, coloured or opaque glass are often found carrying gilt-bronze handles and other such decoration, and reposing upon plinths of semi-precious stone from the Urals or the Altai mountain ranges. Vast porcelain and glass vases were particularly favoured by Catherine the Great.

The story of the Russian goldsmith and the metalworker or foundryman begins in the shadows of pre-recorded history as it does in most countries. The wealth in interest and treasure that come to light when ancient burial sites are excavated reveals that jewellery and metal ornaments were highly prized, and the area of land which is now the RSSR and the Ukranian SSR is rich in such material. When Christianity came to ancient Rus, it was accompanied by many adjuncts to the faith, in addition to which the heavy, strangely austere jewellery which was favoured by the Greeks entranced the Slavs, and Hellenistic fashions spread through the land. Metalwork was richly set with pearls and precious gems in the Byzantine manner. A thorough knowledge already existed in Rus of *niello*, filigree work, and metal-beating, so it was fashion rather than expertise in the crafts that the Russians learned from the Greeks. Icon painting and the art of building in stone and marble were the main skills required and received.

When, like a swarm of locusts, the Golden Horde descended on ancient Rus in the thirteenth century, it destroyed much evidence of a progressive and fascinating past. But Russia's traditional resilience is proverbial. It survived the Tartars as it did the Stalinist purges much later, and not long after the Horde was finally defeated by Ivan IV at the Battles of Kazan and Astrakhan in 1552 and 1556, an English explorer, Richard Chancellor, 'stumbled' on Russia when on his way to find a northern route to Cathay for Elizabeth of England: apparently he was dazzled by the amount of gold plate at a banquet to which he was invited by Ivan the Terrible.

During the reigns of the early Romanov tsars the hallmarking of precious metals had often been haphazardly applied. In *c.* 1700, however, Peter the Great brought in standards and systematic methods for the identification of precious metals in order to rectify these matters.

Foundries had been in existence for many centuries, many of them far away in the distant Ural mountains and safe from the Golden Horde's raiding parties.

Gradually the industry expanded, and by Tsar Peter's reign there were many centres that specialised in wrought and cast iron, and particularly in the production of armaments. It was when Peter the Great closed down the workshops at the Armoury Palace in the Kremlin and partly diverted both men and materials to Tula where he established a munitions factory in 1711, that this became one of the foremost centres for this type of work in early eighteenth-century Russia.

Vast bronze bells, cannon, heavy metal doors and gates, strong boxes and caskets, mantlepieces, as well as wrought-iron and cut-steel furniture, urns, intricate locks and hinges, sabres, swords and rapiers, book, belt and cloak clasps, decorative accoutrements for horses and the most delicate jewellery, were all produced at Tula. *Samovars* – hot-water urns with inbuilt equipment for their heating with charcoal or wood – were an item with which Tula's name became synonymous.

The textiles, embroidery and lace-making industries were also important. Garments were discovered, dating from pre-Christian times, in graves excavated in the Crimea in the 1860s. These were of various colours and embroidered with gold thread.

Linen was among the more important of the textiles produced, and its manufacture can be traced to the twelfth century, as can patterns printed on it using carved wooden blocks and vegetable dyes: this was called the *naboila* method of printing – *nabit* meaning to beat on. Mundane articles such as sheets, bed and wall hangings, tents, curtains and aprons, garments, as well as towels were all made from linens, and towels in Russia carried a certain significance in addition to their obvious use. They were adjuncts to religious worship: they were used for wall decoration and for the covering of hands at ceremonies when bread and salt were presented in welcome: they were placed across the tops of icons (the reason for this custom is uncertain), and upon *analoi* tables supporting them. Towels were used to decorate the 'Red' (or 'beautiful') corner of a room where icons are kept, and also as votive offerings. they were sometimes tied to the branches of trees near churches and cemeteries in honour of departed souls, and also to drape across mirrors so that a new-born soul, in passing, would not take fright at not seeing its own image reflected in them. These ceremonial towels were usually a yard or so long, with heavy, traditional embroidery trimmed with lace at either end.

Embroidery in Russia varied slightly from region to region. Peasant art never came under extraneous, intrusive and possibly more sophisticated influences. It remained simple, colourful, and usually carried ethnic, decorative motifs (i.e. the *Firebird*, the *Petoushok, Sirin* and *Alconist,* geometric patterns, scrolls and flowers), and the most favoured method of work was drawn thread and fine cross-stitching.

The order of colour preference was red, black, yellow, blue (often combined). The more sophisticated work was undertaken in convents (such as the Novodevichi, near Moscow), in schools of embroidery and lace making, and in *terims*. Terims were the womens' quarters in more well-to-do merchants' and nobles' establishments. They should not, however, be confused with harems! Here craftsmanship reached the highest levels of excellence, and superb artifacts were created.

In secular workrooms where garmetns were made and decorated – *kaftans* for men and *sarafans* for women as well as fur-lined *shoushouns* – particular attention was focussed on the *Kokoshnik*. *Kokoshniki* are womens' head-dresses which were worn by peasant and noble women alike, and into the nineteenth century. They were stiffened forms of every shape imaginable, a shape denoting the district from which its wearer came, and were heavily embroidered with the richest materials possible: strings of river-pearls (with which Russia's northern rivers abound,) were often fixed to fall along the wearers' brows and down the sides of the face. In less-monied families beads replaced the pearls. The quality of the furs, jewels and fabrics, naturally, bespeaking a family's status.

Ecclesiastical embroidery at its best was traditionally of unsurpassed workmanship. In early medieval times even the tsaritzas themselves worked on specific articles for the Church: in 1399 the Great Princess Maria of Tver completed and presented a wondrous *plashchenitza* to the Metropolitan at her principality's Cathedral: in later years Tsar Boris Godunov presented the renowned *Pearl Pelena* to act as a veil for Rublev's small icon of the *Old Testament Trinity* at the *Troitza Sergievskaya Lavra* (St Sergius's Monastery of the Holy Trinity round which Zagorsk was built), the seat of the Russian Patriarchate. And there are, of course, other such treasures in the various churches and museums of the Soviet Union.

A particularly interesting subject for the embroiderers' needles was the *pelena*. *Peleny* were icon covers which, very often, carried embroidered versions of the icons they were fashioned to protect: the areas where faces, hands and feet appeared were hand-painted by men since women were not permitted to paint iconographically. On Greek icons only the subjects' faces are left exposed. The *pelena* was the forerunner of the metal *riza*.

The fine stitchery was often quite remarkable for its exactitude in execution. The *peleny*, the *plashchenitzy* (depictions of the *Preparation for the Entombment*), the *nabedrenniki* (symbols of the Church Militant representing the sword and mace), altar frontals cloths for use at altars and vestments all demonstrate this. The interwoven Church-Slavonic lettering which generally surrounds certain depictions, can only be described as wizardry with its close satin-stitch in gold or silver thread. Votive offerings of precious stones and strings of pearls are often found decorating these objects.

INTRODUCTION

Innovations in nineteenth-century Russia were as numerous as in the preceding century. Following the horrific destruction that was inflicted on the country by Napoleon's invasion in 1812, the people rallied, and the mood of national unity created by the war, took root, a new spirit prevailed and the arts returned to their earlier enterprise. Priority, naturally, lay in reparations, with Moscow standing first in line for attention. St Petersburg had suffered no war damage but, despite this, Alexander I's favourite city also received considerable attention from the architects. The days of the grandiose and magnificent palaces however, were over, and building programmes were more prosaic, functional and utilitarian. Architects and designers such as Zakharov (the New Admiralty with its splendid pavilion), Voronykhin (the serenely beautiful Cathedral of the Virgin of Kazan, today's Museum of Atheism), and Stassov (the two Cathedrals for the Preobraj-hensky and the Izmailovsky Regiments) came to the fore. But one man stands out from the others. This was Carlo Rossi (1775–1849), an architect held in high esteem by the Emperor.

The son of an Italian ballerina called Gertrude, and a pupil of another Italian, Vincenzo Brenna (c. 1750–1804, the architect of the moated Mikhailovsky Castle in which Paul I was assassinated), his tastes were in complete accord with those of Alexander who employed hm to help him beautify the city. He was created a member of the powerful Committee for Construction and Hydraulic Works of which he soon became the guiding light, competing with Stassov for work on the more important projects. The immensity of his talent saw him safely through the era in which he worked, namely the change in taste from the neo-Classicism of Alexander's day to that of the neo-Gothic of Nicholas I, but his *rapport* with the new Emperor was not as it had been with the delightful Alexander. Among his more striking constructions were several enchanting bridges and the Mikhai-lovsky Palace (later the Museum of Alexander III and presently the Russian Museum). He supervised the building, sometimes simply the re-fashioning of many exteriors of buildings in the Winter Palace Square, including the layout of the Square itself. He also designed and built the Senate and Synod buildings which he decorated with a great length of Roman frieze in relief sculpture as its entablature, with tall, paired columns and further sculpture to either side and above a triumphal arch. Today it is the repository of the State Archives of the RSSR. Carlo Rossi died of cholera in 1849.

By the second quarter of the nineteenth century the *granite mantle* of which Alexandre Pushkin spoke so eloquently had well and truly descended over St Petersburg. Patriarchal Moscow, however, continued as a predominently wooden city despite its centre which had assumed a similar mantle.

With the accession of Nicholas I (1825–55) Russian tastes in architecture began to turn to the antique as they did in all Europe at that time. The Pan Slav

RUSSIAN RULERS FROM IVAN III

Ivan III	1462–1505
Basil IV	1505–1533
Ivan IV (The Terrible)	1533–1584
Fedor I	1584–1598
Boris Godunov	1598–1605
Fedor II	1605
The Time of Troubles	1605–1613
The ROMANOVS	
Michael	1613–1645
Alexis	1645–1676
Fedor III	1676–1682
Sophia – Regent	1682–1689
Ivan V co-tsars	1682–1689
Peter I co-tsars	1682–1689
Peter I sole tsardom – *Samoderjhavetz*	1689–1725
Catherine I	1725–1727
Peter II	1727–1730
Anna Ioanovna	1730–1740
Ivan VI	1740–1741
Anna Leopoldovna – Regent	1740–1741
Elizabeth	1741–1762
Peter III	1762
Catherine II	1762–1796
Paul	1796–1801
Alexander I	1801–1825
Nicholas I	1825–1855
Alexander II	1855–1881
Alexander III	1881–1894
Nicholas II	1894–1917
The Provisional Government (March–November)	1917
The Bolshevik Revolution (November 6th – Old Style, October 24th – New Style)	1917
The Treaty of Brest Litovsk, December 15th	1917

movement brought the Slavic Revival, and pseudo-medieval buildings began springing up in all directions throughout the land – even the styles of other countries were copied, an example of this being the stables which Nicholas Benois built in the Tudor style at Tsarskoye Selo. In 1896 the architect N.I. Pozdeiev built a house in Moscow for a noble family called Igumnev, and it was a kind of parody of medieval Russian features: today it is the French Embassy. This Slavophilism, together with eclecticism, resulted in the development of a totally new art form – that of the decorator artists who joined the *Mir Iskustva* movement, many of whom came to work for Diaghilev's stable of artists. They, in their turn, were very shortly, if not superseded, then paralleled by the men and women of the *avant garde* – by Tatlin and Malevich. Rodchenko and the Pevsner brothers one of whom was Naum Gabo, Goncharova and Larionov, Kandinsky and Chagall.

Russia's violent and often traumatic history is in strange contrast to the beauty and vitality of her decorative arts. The warmth, humanity, tenacity and resilience of her people lives on, and in this new era of hope and *perestroica* surely a new spirit of creativity will emerge to continue the strongly- identifiable and characteristic arts for which she is famous.

MARINA BOWATER

PLATES

THE DESIGN AND DECORATION OF THE RUSSIAN WRITTEN WORD

The following examples of calligraphy and manuscript ornamentation were collected and researched by Vladimir Stassov. They are part of the illustrative material contained in *Slavonic and Eastern Ornament* which, was published in 1887 in St Petersburg 'with the Imperial permission of Alexander II'. Stassov's text consists mainly of details of the locations of the original manuscripts and the libraries where information about them could be found at the time. Many of these locations, sadly, no longer exist. The plates, however, which are mostly composed of selections of initial letters and decorations from different illuminated manuscripts, provide us with a rare and detailed view of Russian decorative art styles through the centuries, and allow comparison between the work of different regions.

The printing press did not reach Russia until 1553, and the first printed book bears the date 1564. Russia's State Printing Office was established in Moscow by Ivan IV (or 'the Terrible'), but the Kiev Pecherskaya Lavra (the renowned Monastery of the Caves) is known to have produced 24 plates of the Apocalypse in 1646 and 1661, and it also became a great centre for such work.

PLATE 1.

11th century (Kiev).

Drawings and decorations from the Discourse of Gregory the Theologian. Formerly in the Imperial Library, St Petersburg.

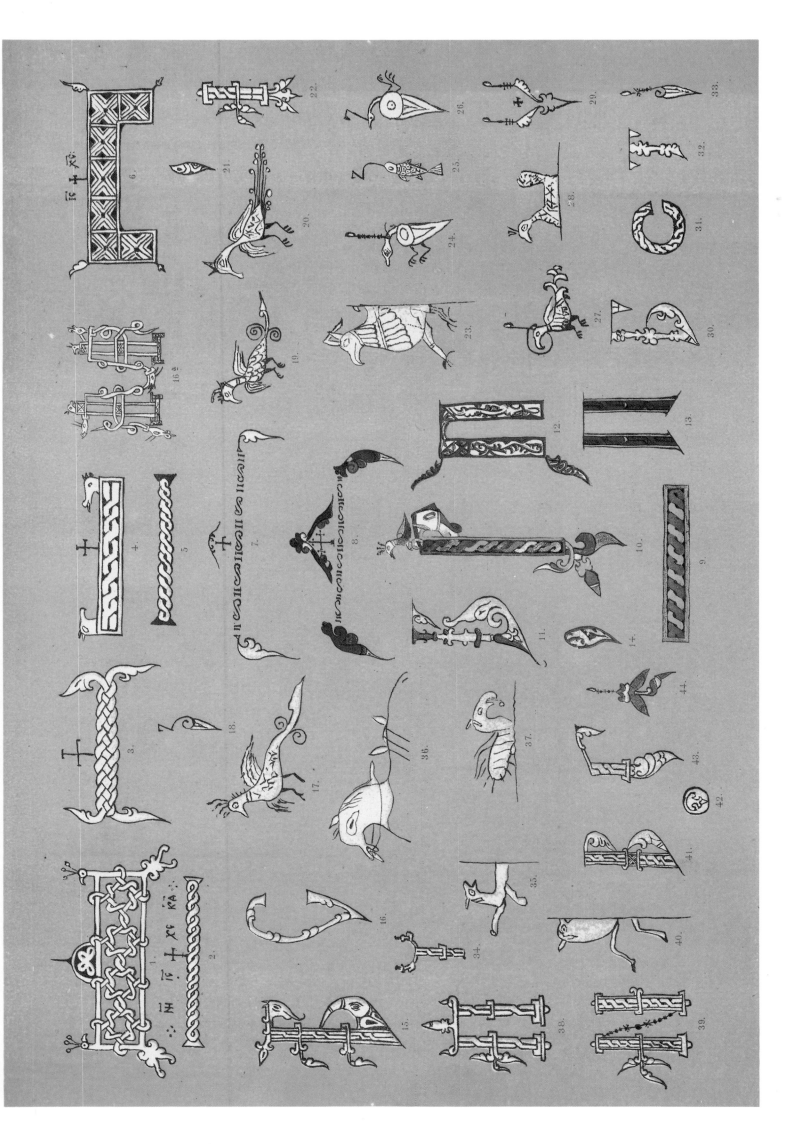

PLATE 2.

11th century (Kiev).

Pandect of Antioch.

From the collection of parchments that were written for Prince Sviatioslav in 1073, and kept at the Library of the Holy Synod, Moscow.

PLATE 3.

11th century (Kiev).

From the collection of Prince Sviatoslav. The gathering of prelates within a fantastic design incorporates many contemporary decorations.

PLATE 4.

12th and 13th centuries
(Kiev and Galitch).

Parchment. Illustrations for a Gospel originally
in the Library of the Holy Synod, Moscow.

Decorations for a Gospel dated 1266. Formerly
in the Imperial Library, St Petersburg.

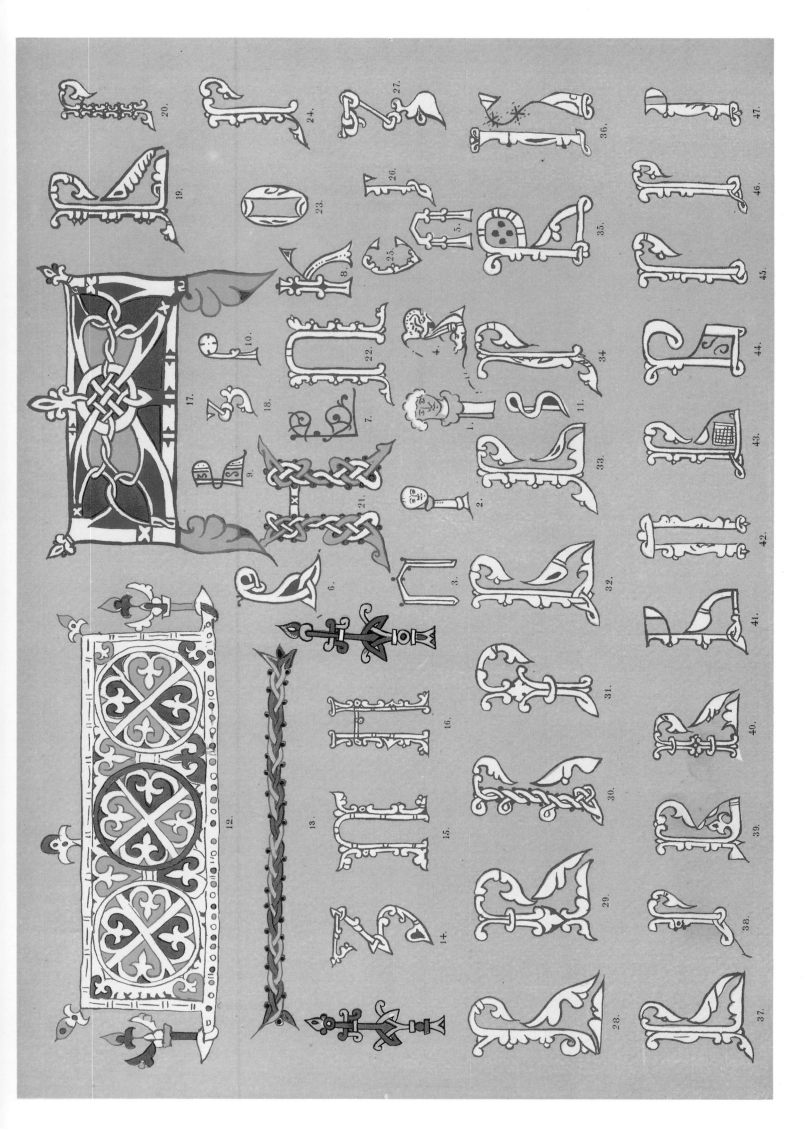

PLATE 5.

15th century (Kiev).

Illustration for a psalter, dated 1397.
Parchment. Detail of a scribe at work, *en
cartouche*, within a fantastic structure which
suggests a church with three cupola. Formerly
in the Museum of the Society of Religious
Bibliophiles at St Petersburg.

PLATE 6.

16th century (Galitch and Wolhynie).

Ornamental material for the Gospels (from
'Peressopnitza'), 1556–61. Parchment, formerly
at the Seminary of Poltava. Painted by Mikhail
Vassievich, son of the priest Sanoka at the
Monastery of the Holy Transfiguration
at Issiaslavl.

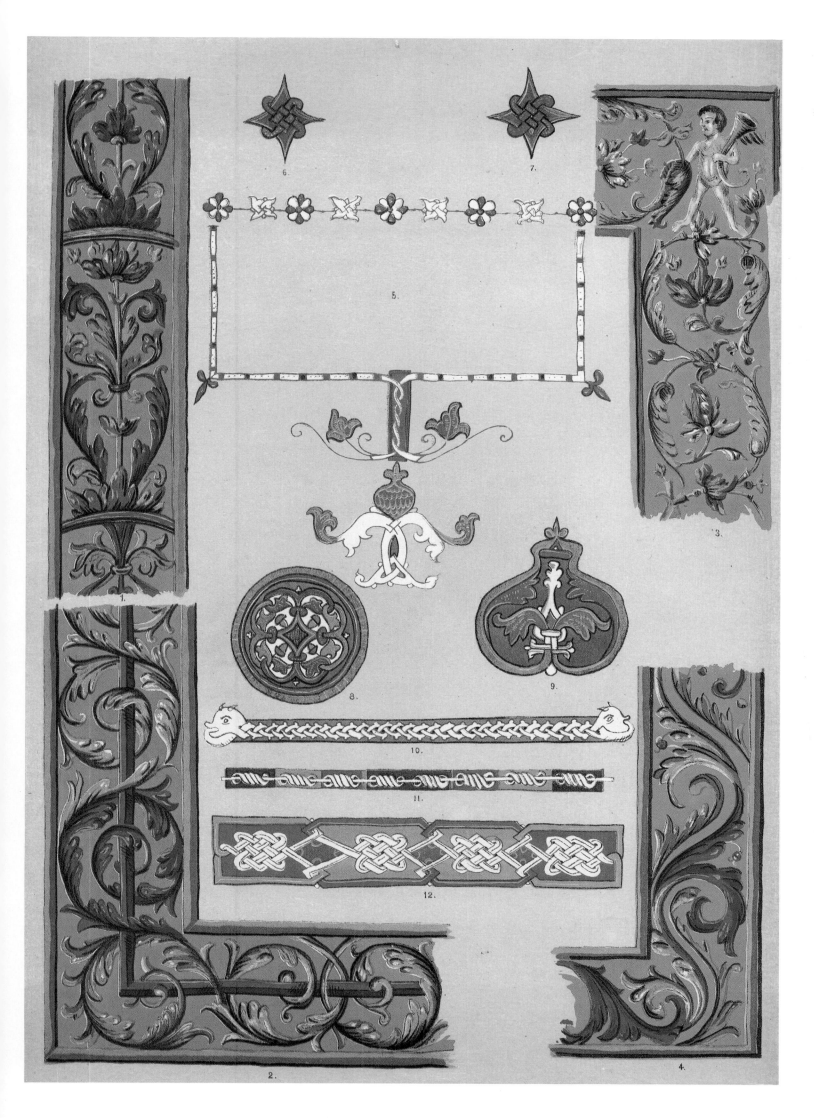

PLATE 7.

16th and 17th centuries
(Galitch and Tchernigov).

From Gospels at the Monastery of Moukatch at
Ougrie: the two upper central strips represent St
Matthew (a man with wings), St Mark (a lion) –
the lower Saint is either Luke or John.
Parchment from the year 1602 originally in the
Imperial Public Library, St Petersburg.

PLATE 8.

11th century (Novgorod).

From St Luke's Gospel 'written' by the scribe Deacon Gregory for the Posadnik Ostromir's edition of the Gospels. Novgorod Cathedral of St Sophia (or Holy Wisdom). 1056–7.

St Luke's symbol, the Bull, is shown descending from a celestrial sphere carrying The Word of God to His Evangelist. The instruments that are laid out with such great precision are those of St Luke's calling – he was an artist and a doctor of medicine.

PLATE 9.

11th century (Novgorod).

Examples of 11th-century Novgorodian
manuscript illumination.

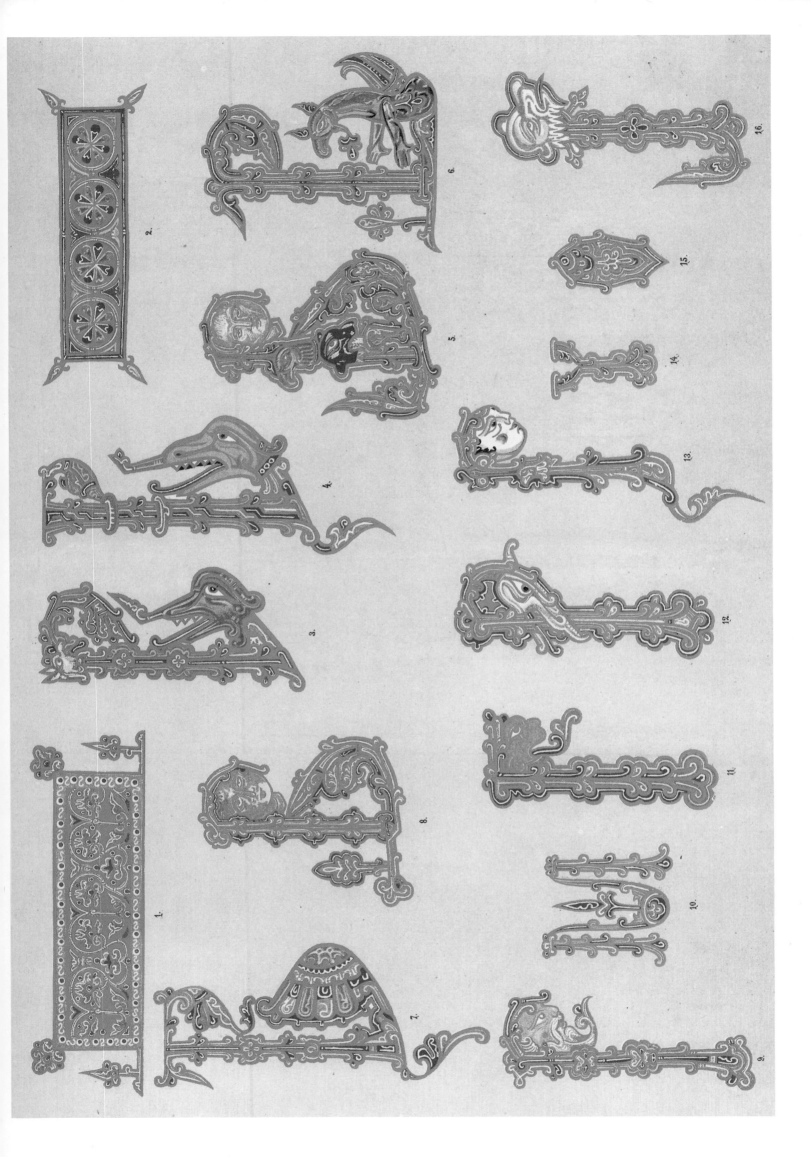

PLATE 10.

11th and 12th centuries (Novgorod).

Detail for menological (May) writings.
Parchment. Formerly in the Cathedral of St
Sophia, Novgorod.

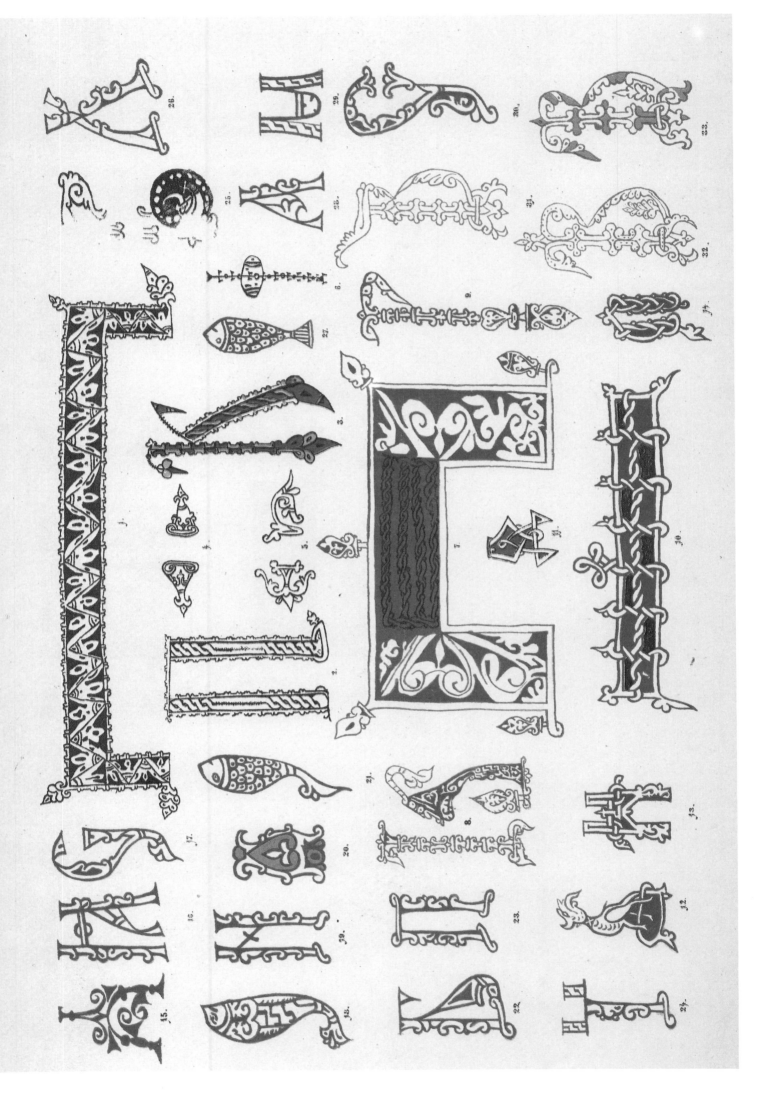

PLATE 11.

11th and 12th centuries (Novgorod).

Decoration from a psalter. Many of the letters
are recognisable today.

PLATE 12.

11th century (Novgorod).

From the Gospel at the Youriev Monastery written by Fedor of Ougra, 1120–28 for the monastery of St George at Novgorod. The drawing represents a church with apertures left blank for icons or lettering.

PLATE 13.

12th century (Novgorod).

Examples of Novgorodian calligraphy by Feodor of Ongra from Gospels at the Youriev Monastery.

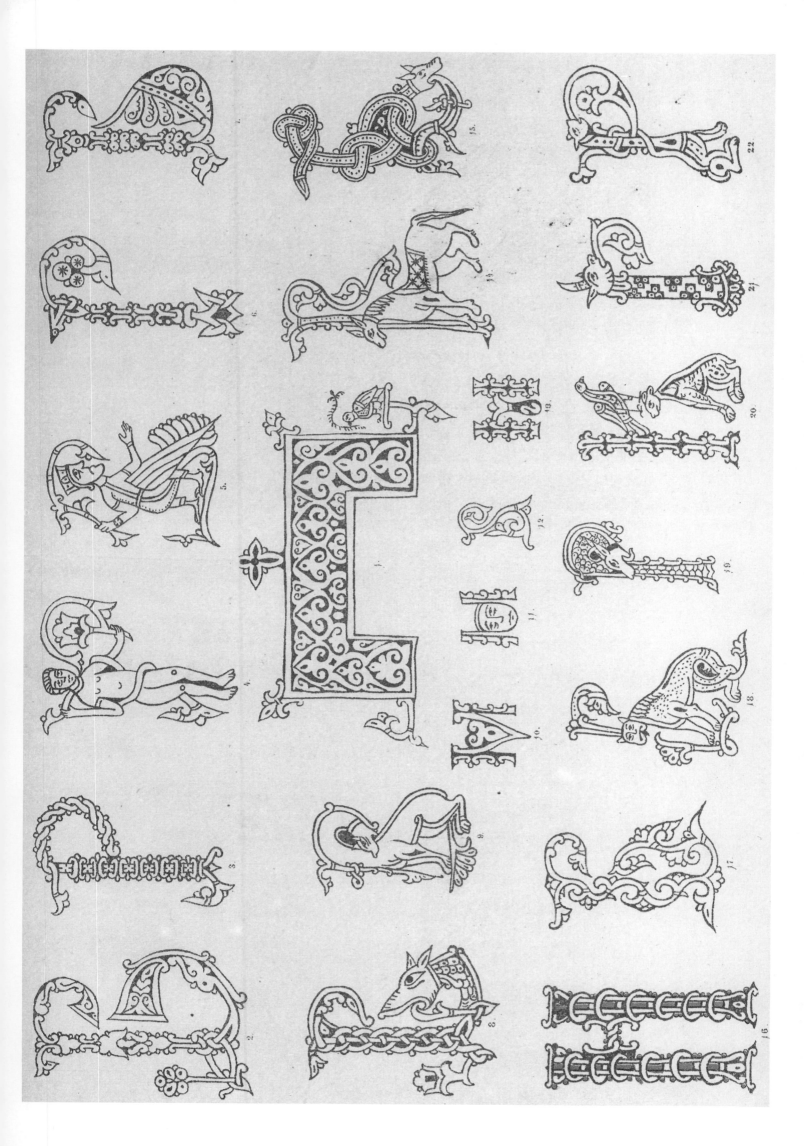

PLATE 14.

12th century (Novgorod).

Examples of Novgorodian calligraphy by
Feodor of Ongra from Gospels at the Youriev
Monastery.

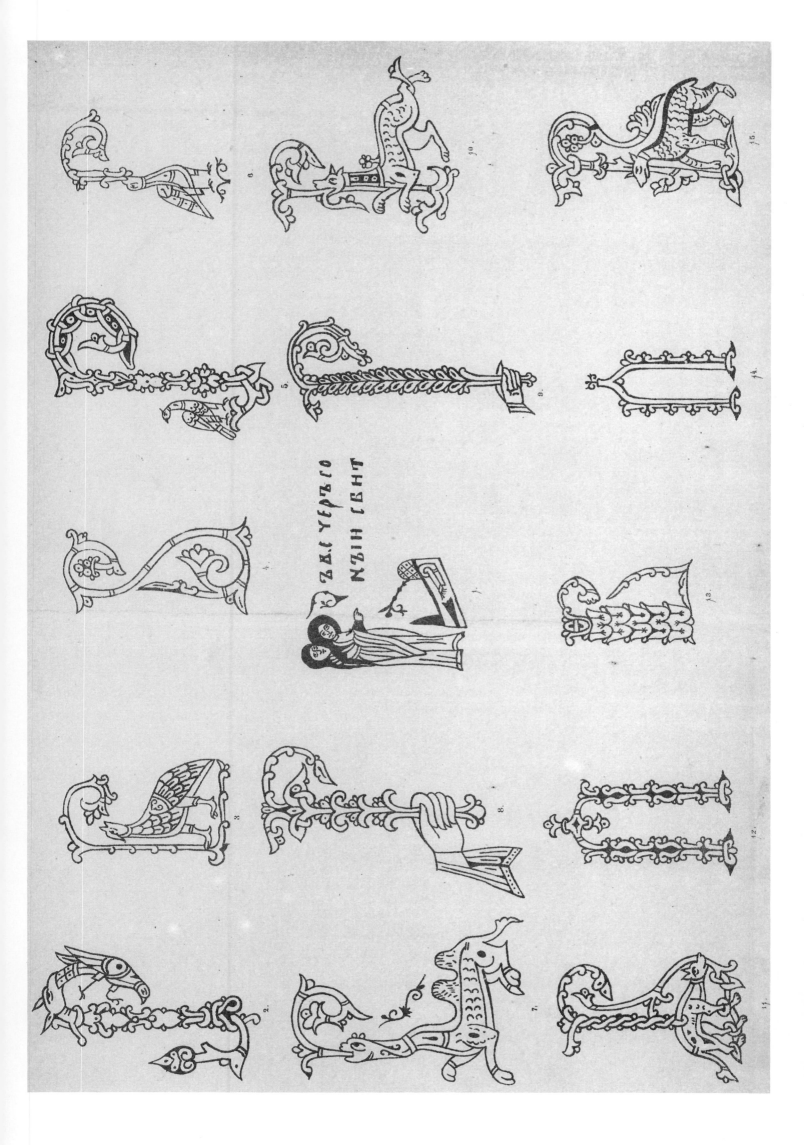

PLATE 15.

12th century (Novgorod).

Calligraphy and ornamentation for the Gospel
of Mstislav, *c.* 1120. Formerly in the Cathedral
of the Archangel at Moscow. 'Written' for
Mstislav by Alexis, son of the priest, Lazar.
Parchment.

PLATE 16.

12th century (Novgorod).

Gospel dated 1164. Parchment. Formerly in the Moscow Public Library of Roumianzev. 'Written' by the clerk of the Church of the Apostle Konstantin ('in life', Dobrilov). The *kavcheg* (an icon container) is surmounted by a cupol and two fabulous birds.

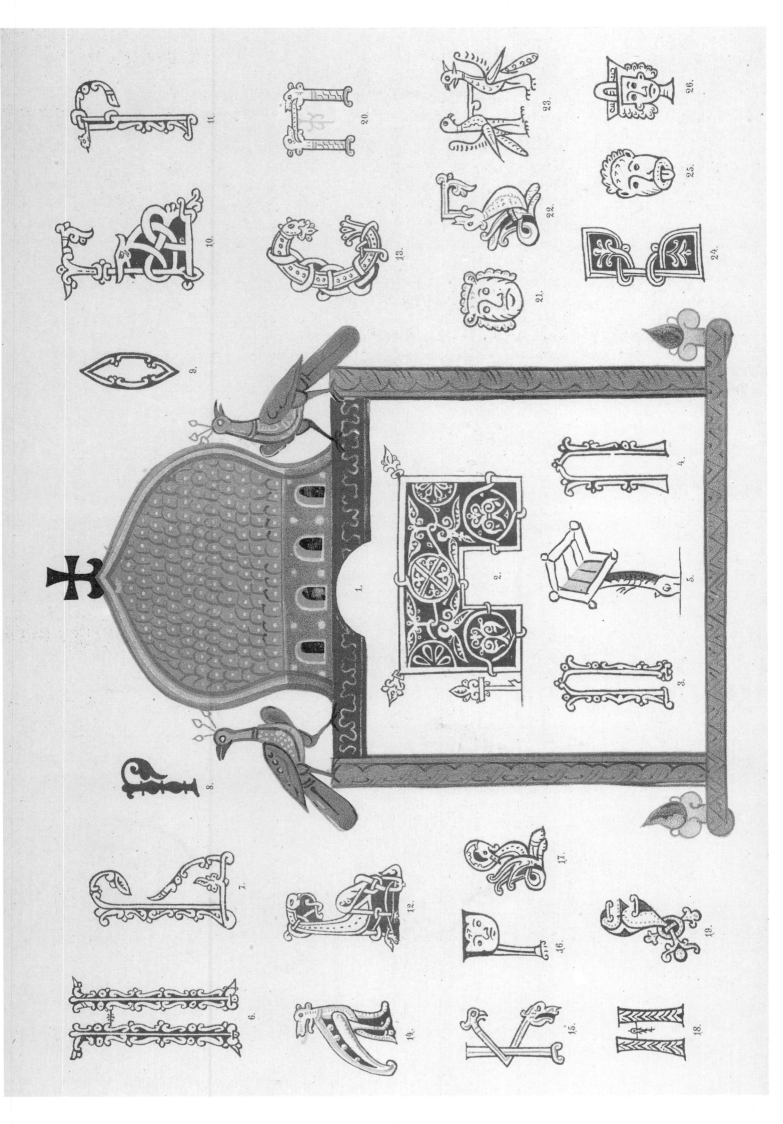

PLATE 17.

12th and 13th centuries (Novgorod).

Decoration for the Book of Offices of Varlaam
of Khoutine. Parchment.

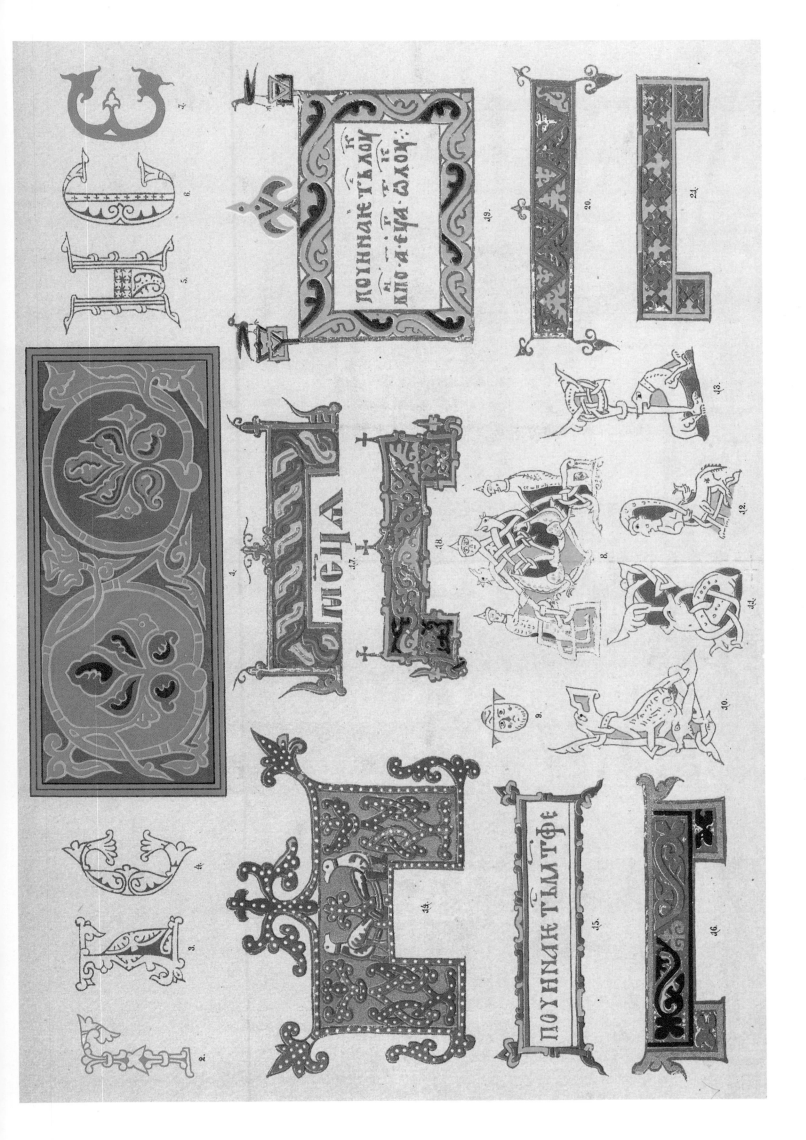

PLATE 18.

12th and 13th centuries (Novgorod).

Novgorodian sense of colour predominates in these examples of calligraphic style. Parchment. From a Gospel originally in the Cathedral of the Archangel, Moscow.

PLATE 19.

12th and 13th centuries (Novgorod).

Calligraphy and ornamentations for a
hermeneia with names. Parchment. From the
library of the Monastery of the New Jerusalem
near Moscow.

The 13th-century Panteleimonsky Gospels.
Parchment. Worked on by Maxim Tochinitz at
the Church of St John the Baptist, Novgorod.
This style of calligraphy was also used on the
13th-century psalter at the Nereditza (a church
destroyed by enemy action in World War II).
The psalter, however, was rescued, and is now
at the St Petersburg Spiritual Academy.

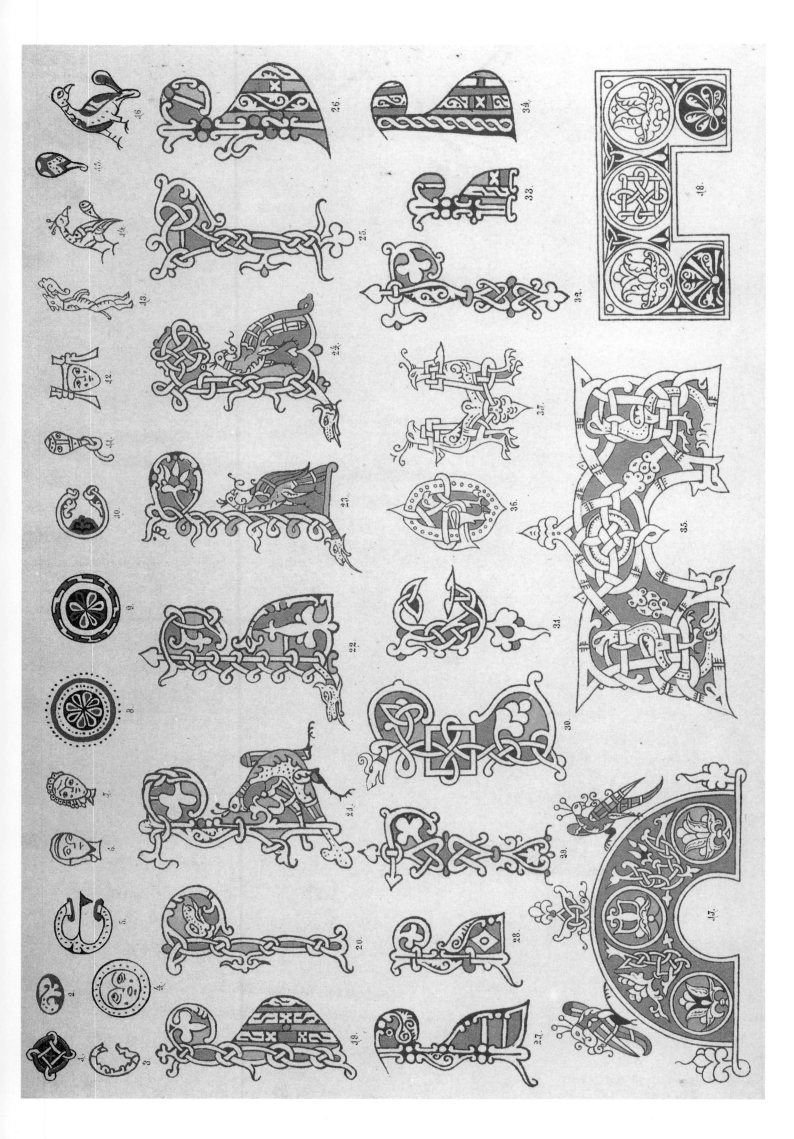

PLATE 20.

13th century (Novgorod).

Calligraphy and a stylised church which
decorate St Luke's Acts of the Apostles. From
St Joseph's Volokhlamsky Monastery.

PLATE 21.

13th century (Novgorod).

Imaginative calligraphy used in a Gospel
produced in 1270. Parchment.

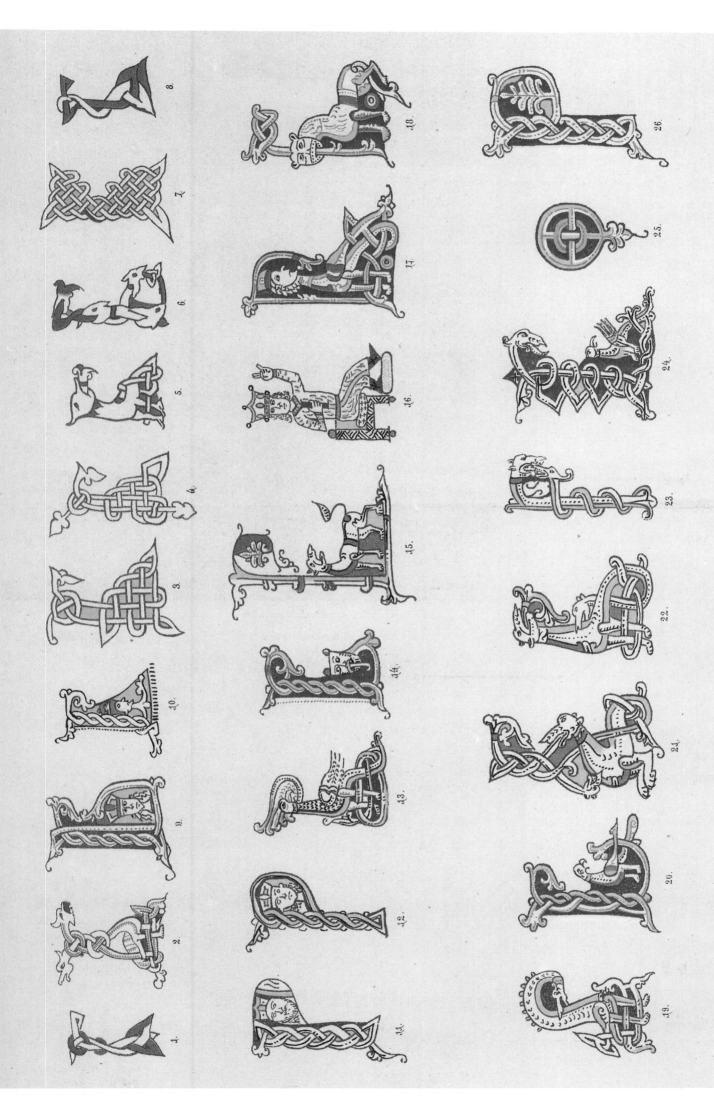

PLATE 22.

13th century (Novgorod).

Calligraphy for Gospels. Parchment formerly in
the St Petersburg Public Library.

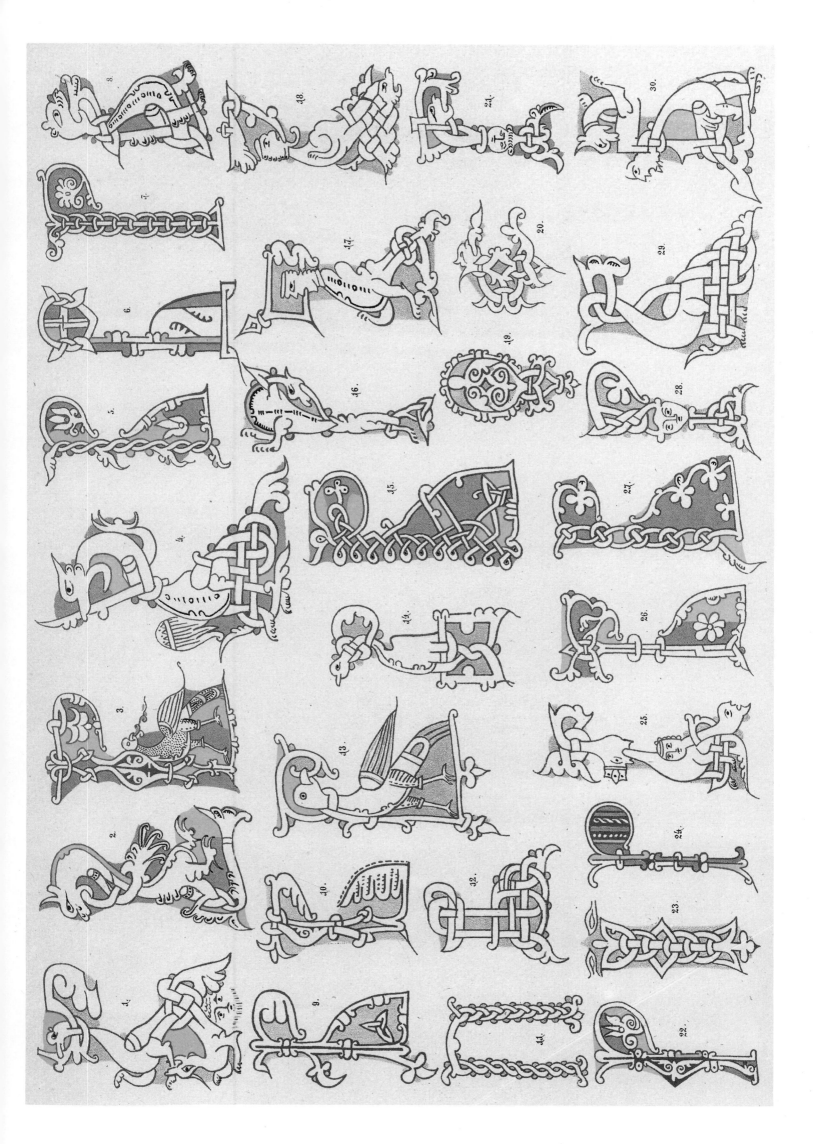

PLATE 23.

14th century (Novgorod).

From a Gospel. Parchment formerly at the
Imperial Library of Sciences, St Petersburg

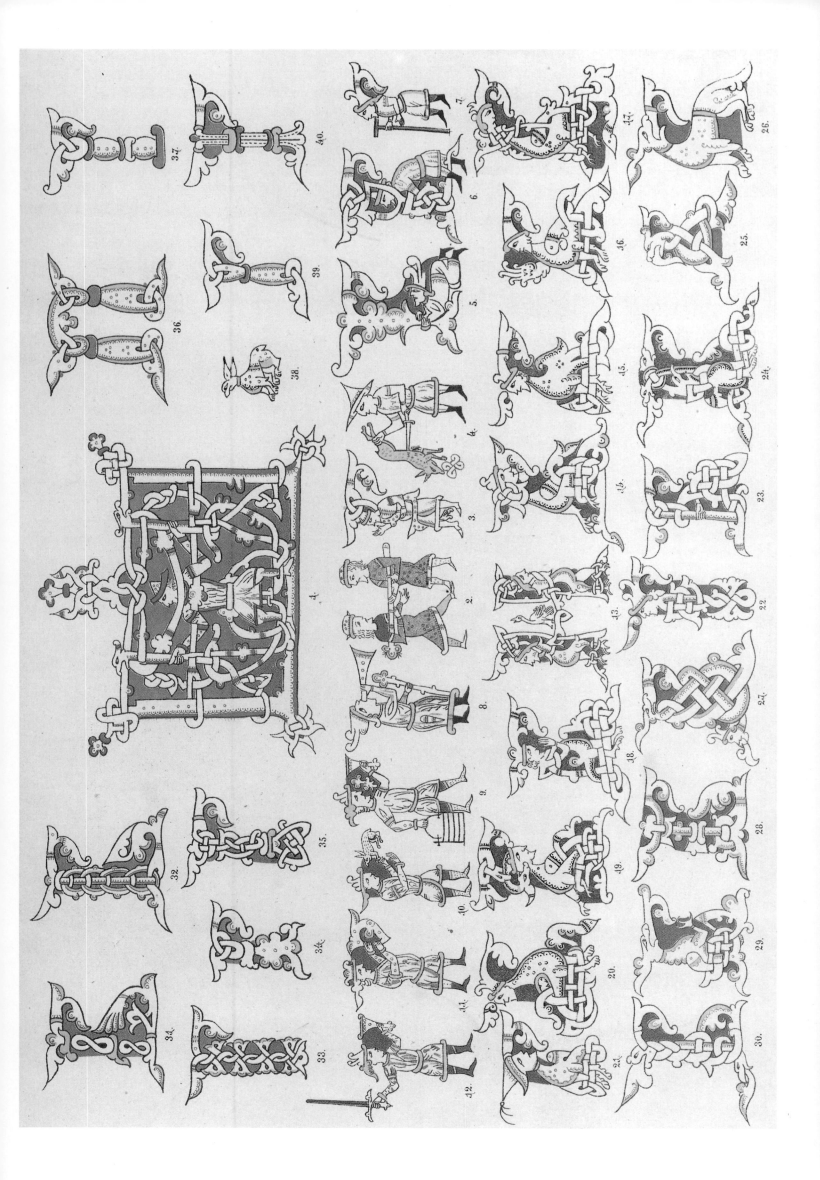

PLATE 24.

14th century (Novgorod).

A depiction of some uncanonical Tsar Gates,
also some calligraphy painted in a similar style
for psalters. Parchment.

PLATE 25.

14th century (Novgorod).

The calligraphy here is of particular interest as it
incorporates human figures wearing
contemporary dress. From a psalter.
Parchment.

PLATE 26.

14th century (Novgorod).

Psalter. Parchment in the Imperial Public
Library, St Petersburg. The central features are
the open Tsar Gates of an *iconostasis* (a screen
that separates the sanctuary from the nave
of a church).

PLATE 27.

14th and 15th centuries (Novgorod).

Prologues. Parchments from the Library of the
Holy Synod at Moscow. A fantastic winged
figure has no known symbolism.

PLATE 28.

15th and 16th centuries (Novgorod).

A 15th-century hermeneia on parchment formerly in the Library of Topography at the Holy Synod, Moscow. From the library of the Reverend Amphilokhi, the Danilov Monastery, Moscow. A church is portrayed within which are Tsar Gates.

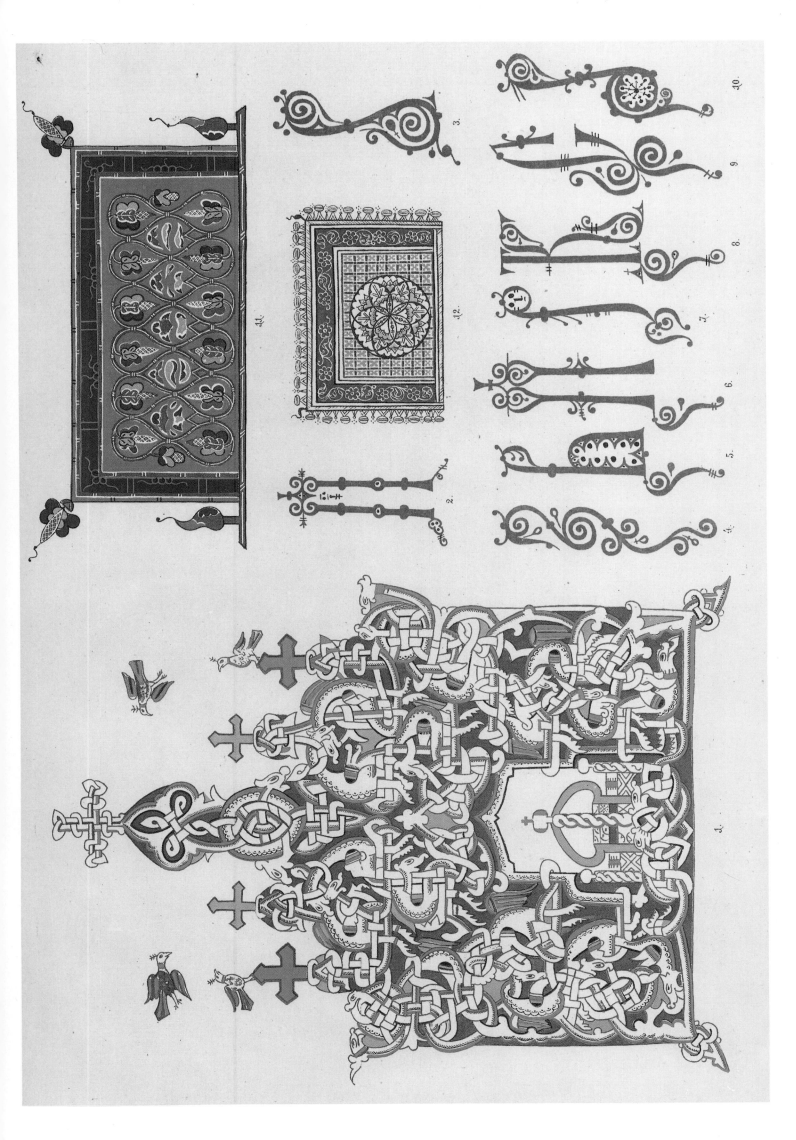

PLATE 29.

14th and 15th centuries (Pskov).

Pskovian calligraphic workmanship was very similar to that of Novgorod. The Gospels and psalters were decorated with much the same ethnic forms, and the decorated chapter headings were of a similar style.

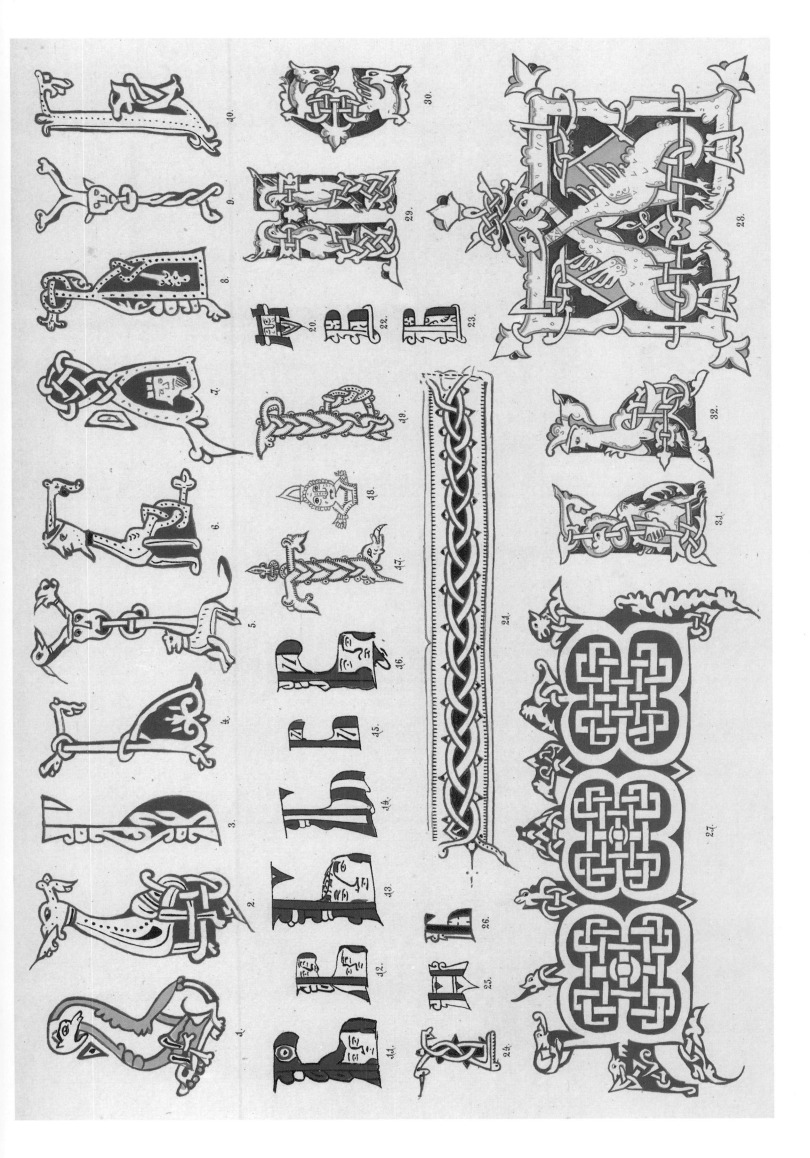

PLATE 30.

15th century (Pskov).

The illustrations contained in this plate were
created for Gospels produced in the year 1409.
Parchment. Formerly in the Library of the Holy
Synod, Moscow. A menology dated 1413.
Parchment, formerly in the Library of the Holy
Synod, Moscow. A prologue for the year 1425.
Parchment, formerly in the Library of the Holy
Synod, Moscow. Written by Daniel, a prelate at
the church of St Mikhail.

PLATE 31.

15th and 16th centuries
(Belozersk).

Fine decorative and ornamental work on paper
for Gospels. Formerly in the Library of St
Petersburg's Spiritual Academy.

PLATE 32.

16th and 17th centuries
(Belozersk).

The designs that are shown here are from the
Acts of the Apostles and the Gospels. Formerly
in the Monastery of Kiril–Belozersky's library,
and in the Library of St Petersburg's
Spiritual Academy.

PLATE 33.

14th and 15th centuries
(Polodsk, Grodno)

Decorative images taken from Gospels formerly
in the Imperial Library at St Petersburg, No. 17,
f, parchment. From the many annotations on
this MS it is evident that the Gospels were once
the property of the Church of St John the
Baptist on the island of Polodsk.

A service book for the Liturgy during Lent
1466. Formerly in the Imperial Public Library at
St Petersburg. No. 125, f°, paper. Written by
the Deacon Evstaoi at Grodna, for the
Cathedral of the Mother of God by order of
Fedor Volovich.

Further ornamentations from 14th- and 15th-
century Gospels. Formerly in the public library
at Vilno.

PLATE 34.

15th–16th centuries
(Grodno, Poltozk, Kovel,
Viazma, Vilno).

Illustrations taken from the 15th-century gospel
named 'of Volkovyskoye', and other religious
books. The originals formerly in the library of
the Holy Synod, Moscow, and the Imperial
Public Library, St Petersburg.

PLATE 35.

15th and 17th centuries (Smolensk Sloutzk).

Several magnificent ornamental studies for illustrating religious texts, in this case, The Four Evangelists. Formerly in the Library of the Holy Synod, Moscow.

PLATE 36.

18th century (Nijni-Novgorod).

Illustrations taken from a book containing a collection of liturgical offices. Previously in the private collection of A. Titoff of Rostov Yaroslavlsky. It was written at the small and secluded monastery of Osinovsk in the government ('county') of Nijni-Novgorod, the district of Semonov, by the hand of the Venerable Gregory.

PLATE 37.

13th–15th centuries (Tver).

Decorative calligraphy from the Chronicle of
Georgi Amartol, 13th century, at the Spiritual
Academy of Moscow located at St Sergius's
Monastery of the Holy Trinity. No. 100, f°,
parchment. And as it is found in the *Pateric*
(lives of the Fathers) at the Kievan Monastery of
the Caves. Imperial Public Library of St
Petersburg No. 31, 4°, parchment. This book
was produced in the reign of the Great Prince
Ivan Mikhailovich, by order of the Bishop
Arsenii of Tver.
Gospels dated 1417. At the Library of the
Cathedral of the Transfiguration at Tver, 4°,
paper. Written at Tver at the Church of the
Saviour at the time of the Great Prince Ivan
Mikhailovich, by order of the Bishop Anthony
of Tver, by the hand of Ilya.

PLATE 38.

16th century (Tver).

A prologue dated 1521. From the Imperial Public Library at St Petersburg. No. 624, paper. This book was presented to the Church of SS. Flor and Lavr at the time of the rule of the Great Prince Vassili Ioanovich, under the Governor of Tver, Prince Mikhail Dannilievich, by order of Fedor Davydov, the son of Chebotinkov. From Pogodin's collection. And another from the collection of Count Tolstoy – No. 103, paper.

PLATE 39.

15th century (Ouglitch).

Calligraphy from a Psalter dated 1485. At the Imperial Public Library of St Petersburg. No. 5 (32), 1°, paper. Written in the town of Ouglitch at the time of the Great Princes Ivan Vassilievich and Andrei Vassilievich, and of Bishop Asaph by the priest Fedor, the son of Klementi Sharapoff. Formerly in the collection of Count Tolstoy.

Note the bell-ringer (left).

PLATE 40.

15th–17th centuries
(Kolomna, Jaroslavl, Sviajsk).

From a prologue dated 1481. Formerly in the Imperial Public Library, St Petersburg. No. 311 (85), f°, paper. Written by order of the Archimandrite at the Spasky Monastery at Kolomna, by the prelate Fedot and the Deacon Semon. From the collection of Count Tolstoy.

Gospels dated 1509, in the Imperial Public Library at St Petersburg. No. 132, 4°, paper. Written by the priest Daniel. From the collection of Pogodine.

Synodkon of the year 1656. At the Library of the Archipiscopy of Jaroslavl, No. 1058, f°, paper. Also a 15th century *Menee* (monthly calendar of saints) formerly in the Library of the Holy Synod, Moscow. No. 522, f°, paper. Originally at the Monastery of the Mother of God at Svijsk.

PLATE 41.

16th–17th centuries
(Nijni Novgorod).

Illustrations from Gospels dated 1551. Imperial Public Library, St Petersburg, No. 37 (180), f° Paper. Written by the priest Adrian, in the reign of the pius Tsar Ivan Vassilievich of all the Russias, by order of the Monastery of St Makarii Theltovodsky's abbot. From Count Tolstoy's collection.

A collection of 18th-century manuscripts of Holy Offices. In the library of A. Titoff at Rostov Jaroslavsky. No. 2533, 8°, paper. Written at the Ossinovsky Hermitage, in the district of Semonovsk, by the hand of the Venerable Gregori.

PLATE 42.

15th and 16th centuries (Moscow).

Acts of the Apostles, 1389–1425. Private collection. Parchment. This book was written at the time of the Great Prince Vassili Dmitievich, and the Archbishop Kiprian of all the Russias by Kouziemka, a prelate at the Church of the Elevation of the Cross.

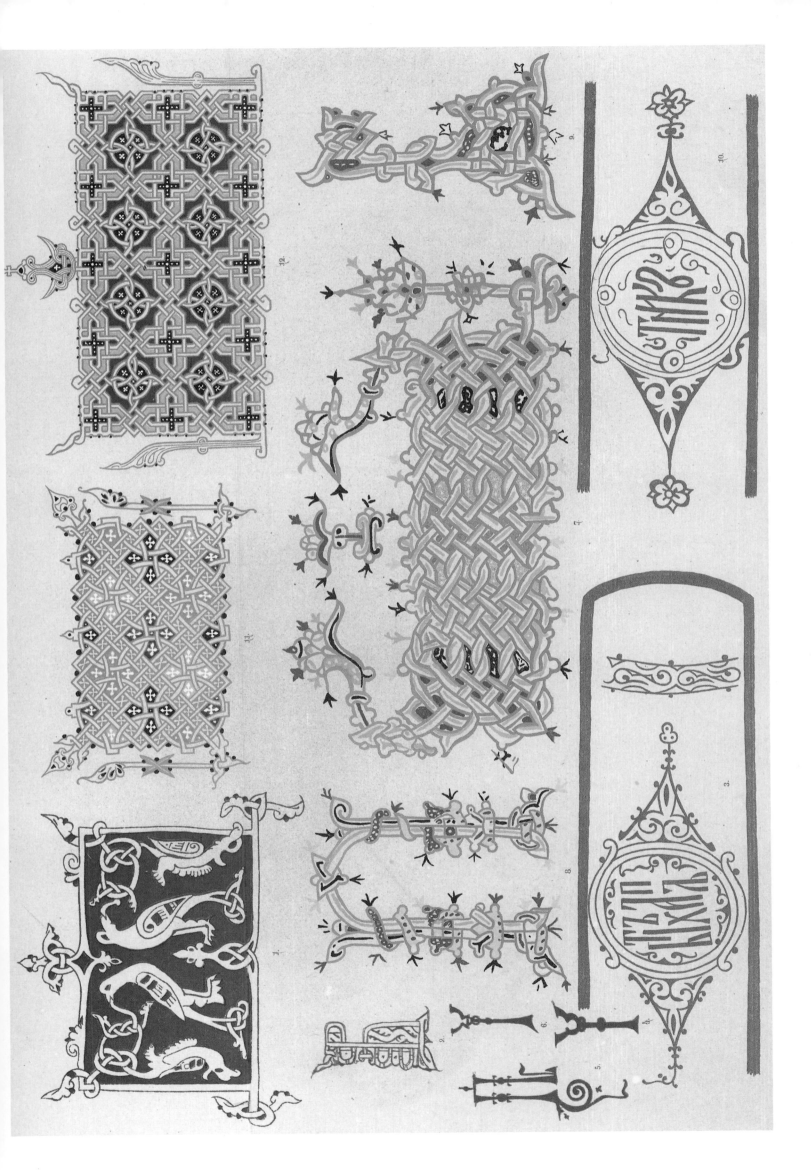

PLATE 43.

15 century (Moscow).

From the Gospels. Formerly in the Library of
the Moscow Spiritual Academy. Paper.

Psalter with 15th-century prayers. Paper.
Formerly in the Troitza Sergievskaya Lavra,
near Moscow.

PLATE 44.

15th and 16th centuries (Moscow).

Psalter with 15th-century prayers. Paper.
Formerly in the Troitza Sergievskaya Lavra (St
Sergius's Monastery of the Holy Trinity),
near Moscow.

Chronology for the year 1485. Paper. The
Public and Roumianzev Museum, Moscow.

The Four Evangelists. Paper.
The Tver Museum.

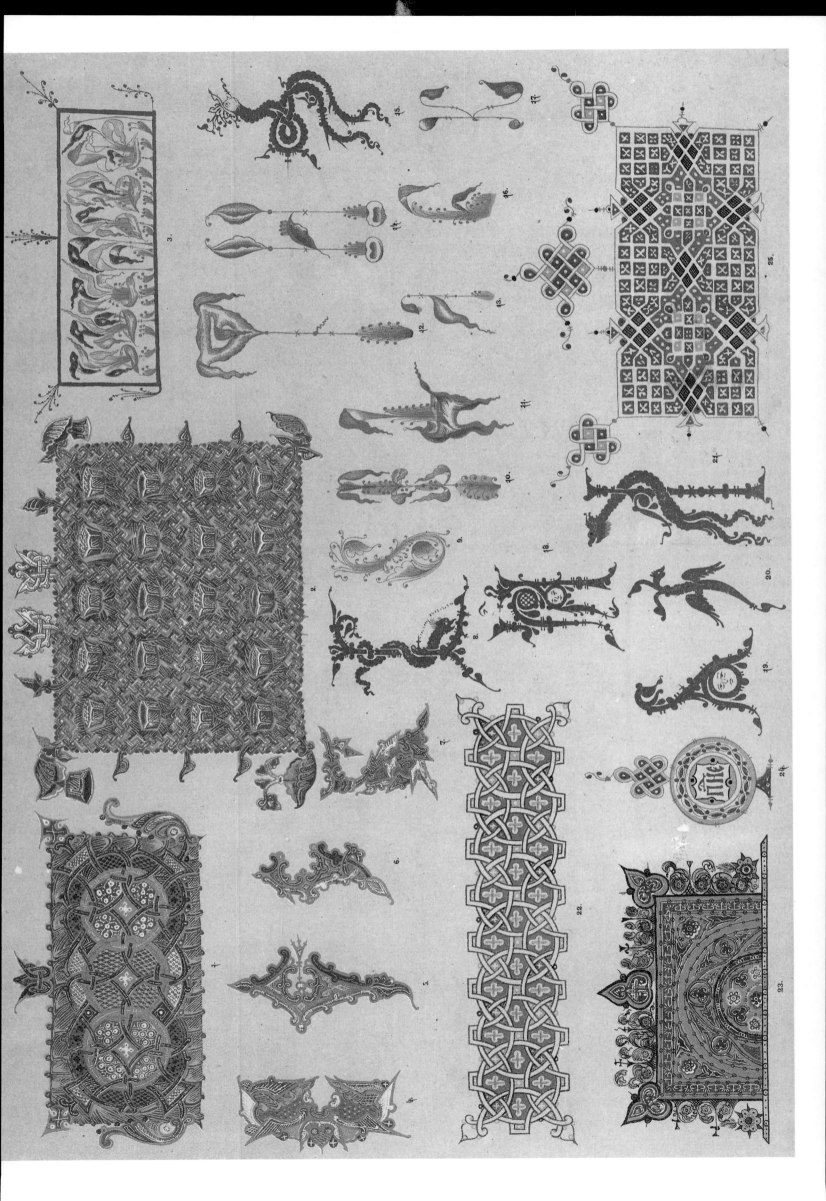

PLATE 45.

16th century (Moscow).

From Gospels formerly in the library of the
Convent of St Sergius's the Holy Trinity.

PLATE 46.

16th century (Moscow).

From Gospels dated 1531, formerly in the Library of the Convent of St Sergius's the Holy Trinity. No. 9, fᵒ, paper. Written by the priest, Bireff.

Examples of calligraphy from further numerous Gospels, manuscripts and papers, including a missive of Tsar Ivan the Terrible of 1571, to the Monastery of Khilandre (Mount Athos): fᵒ. Parchment. From the copy of the facsimile in the collection of the Bishop Porphyre, formerly in the Imperial Public Library, St Petersburg.

PLATE 47.

16th–17th centuries (Moscow).

Book of songs ('hymnal'), 16th century,
formerly in the Imperial Public Library at St
Petersburg, No. 184, 4°, paper. Material taken
from various Gospels, psalters, scripts, and
from the work of St John of Damascus dated
1673 provide examples of calligraphy of
particular interest.

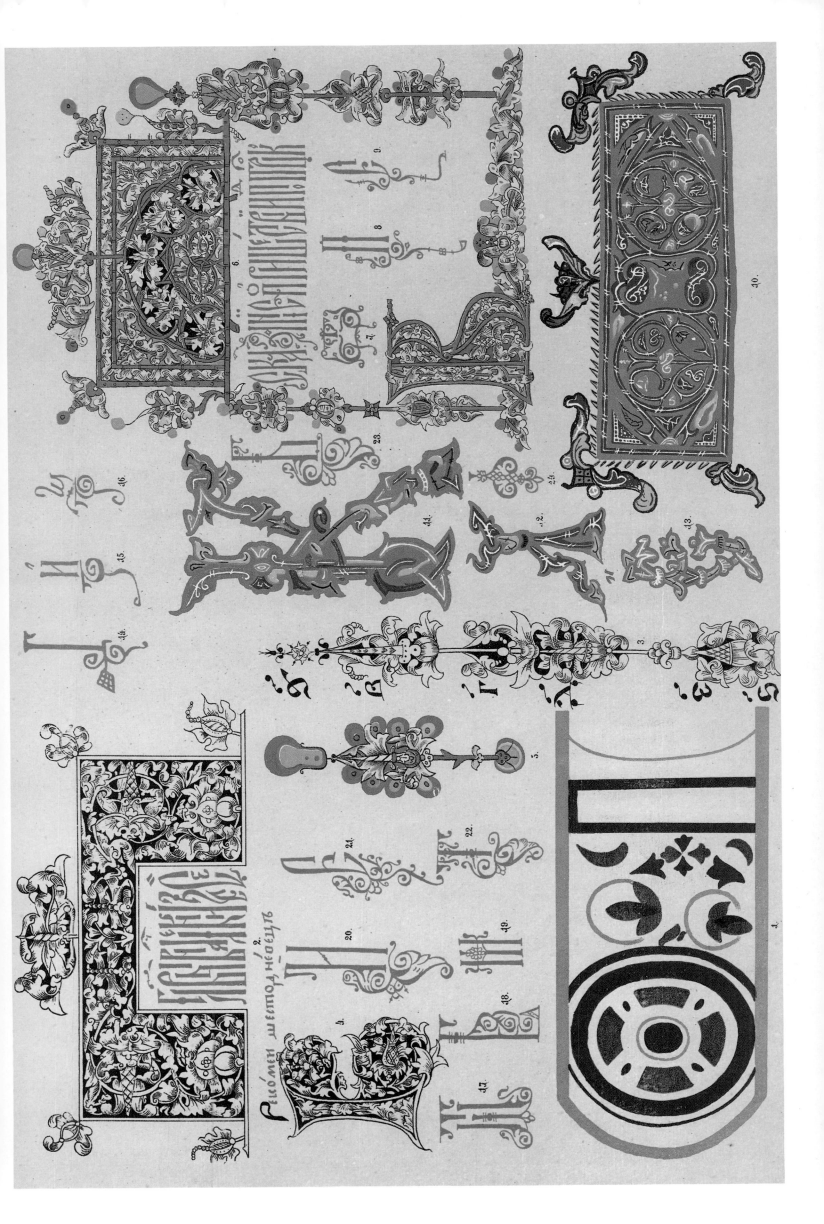

PLATE 48.

17th century (Moscow).

Illustrations taken from *The Book of Sybils* dated 1672. Formerly in the keeping of the Public and Roumianzeff Museum, Moscow.
No. 227. Paper.

The Boroniev Chronicle of 1689. Formerly in the Public and Roumianzeff Museum, Moscow.
No. 15. Paper.

Acathist (a series of prayers) to the Mother of God, written by Karion Ustomin for the Tsaritza Prasceva Fedorovna.

PLATE 49.

10th–12th centuries (Armenia).

Ornamentation taken from the four Gospels 'of Trebizond'. At the library of the Monastery of Mekhiterists on the island of St Lazar, near Venice. Parchment. 10th century.

Ornamentation from the four Gospels dated 1193. Formerly in the library of the Monastery of Mekhiterists on the island of St Lazar, near Venice. No 196 (20), 4°, parchment. Written by the monk Hachatur, designed by Vard.

The four Gospels, 12th century. Formerly in the library of Professor N.O. Émin, Moscow. Parchment.

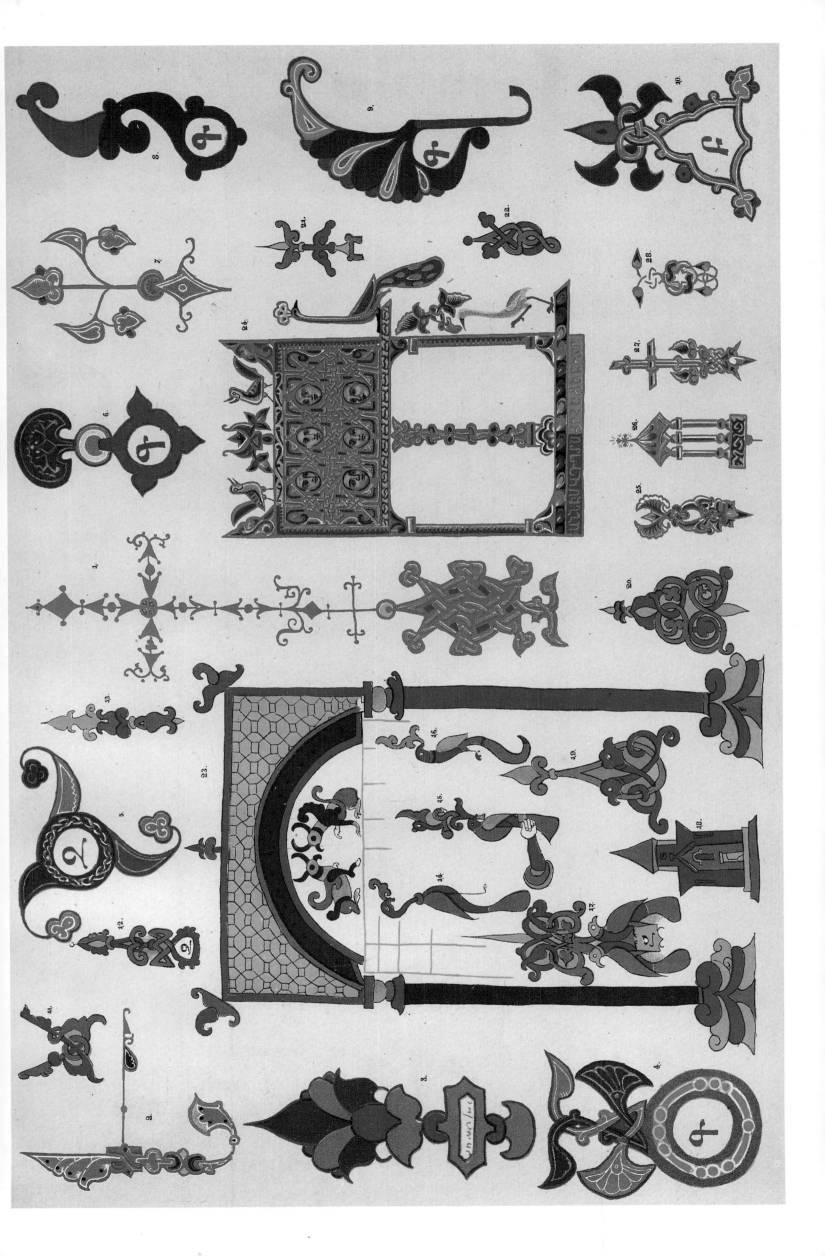

PLATE 50.

12th–13th centuries (Armenia).

The four Gospels, dated 1193. From the Library
of Mekhiterists on the island of St Lazar, near
Venice: No. 1635 (40), 4°. Parchment. This
work was executed by the celebrated designer
Konstantin for the Monastery of Skevra near
Lambron, in Sicily which was under the
Patriarch Gregory, and the Sicilian
Bishop Nersès.

PLATE 51.

13th century (Armenia).

Ornament taken from the four Gospels, dated 1200. Formerly in the library of the Monastery of the Mekhiterists on the island of St Lazar, near Venice. No. 1366 (39), 4°. Cotton paper. Written by one, Basil.

The four Gospels, 1193. Library of the Monastery of the Mekhiterists on the island of St Lazar, near Venice. Written by the celebrated scribe Konstantin for the Church of the Saviour at the Monastery of Skevra near Lambron, in Sicily, in the jurisdiction of the Patriarch Gregory and the Sicilian Bishop, Nersès.

An ornament from a book on the Life of Alexander the Great: 13th century. Formerly in the library of Mekhiterists on the island of St Lazar, near Venice. No. 424, f°. Cotton paper. King Darius reading a letter to his generals.

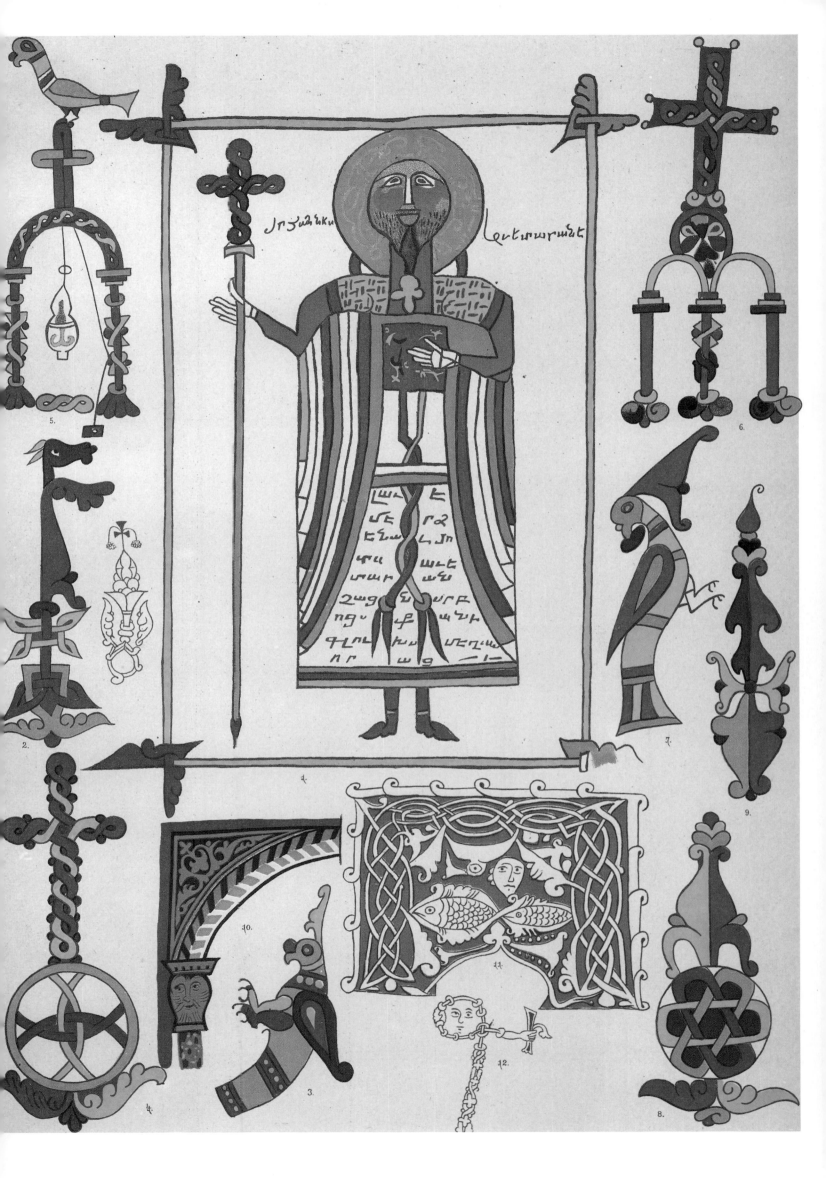

PLATE 52.

13th century (Armenia).

Ornament taken from the four Gospels, dated
1244. Formerly in the library of the Monastery
of the Mekhiterists on the island of St Lazar,
near Venice. No. 69 (66), 4°. Parchment.
Written at Roumkal on the Euphrates, the
residence of the Patriarch Kupakos, by order of
the Catholicos Konstantin I.

Marginal ornaments from 10th-century
Trebizondian Gospels at St Lazar.
Ornament taken from St Mark's Gospel, dated
1274, in the Bibliotèque Nationale, Paris. No.
12, 4°. Cotton paper. Written by Stephan
Yeretzorty for the Tsaritza Kiria Anna, also
called Théophanon, the wife of King Léon III
of Sicily.

PLATE 53.

14th century (Armenia).

Sharaknotz (a book of prayer with chant) dated
1341. Bibliothèque National, Paris. Written by
the copyist Avétikh under the patronage of a
lady called Tadj, and illuminated by an artist
called Jean under the patronage of the
priest Adéodat.

From 14th-century Gospels in the Royal
Library, Berlin. No. 272, 4°. Cotton paper.
From the collection of Minutoli.

PLATE 54.

14th–18th centuries (Armenia).

The four Gospels formerly in the private collection of His Imperial Majesty the Emperor of Russia. Small, 4°. Parchment. This manuscript was presented to the Emperor Alexander II on the 19th February, 1880, the 25th anniversary of his reign by the Patriarch Etschmiadzin.

Some further decoration from the four Gospels dated 1707. Royal Library, Berlin. No. 337, 4°. Cotton paper.

PLATE 55.

14th–17th centuries (Armenia).

From 15th-century Psalter in the Bibliotèque
Nationale de Paris. No. 1, 4°. Parchment.
Written by a priest named Nersès.
Ornamentation illustrated from certain other
texts. The central picture illustrates The
Last Judgement.

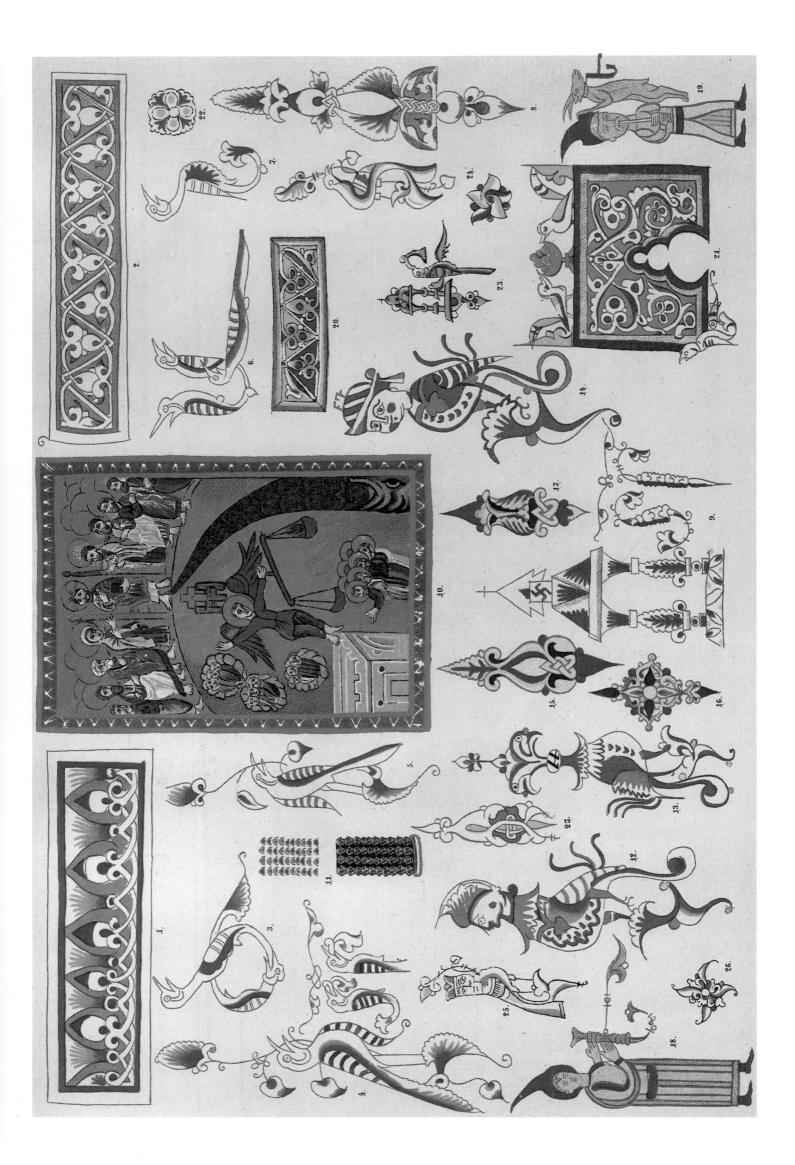

PLATE 56.

16th–17th centuries (Armenia).

Ornamentation from a 16th-century
Sharakonotz (prayer book) formerly in The
Imperial Public Library, St Petersburg. Also
from 12th-century Gospels at the Bibliotèque
National de Paris. Comment on the Proverbs of
Solomon, 17th century, probably written
by Konstantin.

Also, ornaments taken from the four Gospels.
17th century. In the Bibliotèque National
de Paris.

The four Gospels dated 1635. Formerly in the
library of A. Zwenigossky, St Petersburg.
'Written by the hand of the sinner, Isaac (Sahak)
at Baghesh (near Lake Van), at the time of
Philip, the most holy Catholicos.'

PLATE 57.

9th–11th centuries (Georgia).

Liturgy from the collection of the
Bishop Porphyre.

Illustration from the life of St John Chrysostom
from the year 968. Formerly in the Imperial
Public Library of St Petersburg. Small, 4°.
Parchment. Written at the Monastery of
Chariton at Mount Sinai by John Sapareli, at the
request of Mikhail Panaskerteli. From the
collection of the Bishop Porphyre.

The Four Evangalists dated 995. Imperial Public
Library of St Petersburg. No. 212, 4°.
Parchment. Written at the Cathedral of the
Holy Apostles at Tbeti (in 'the province of
Batoum'), in the reign of David Kouropalata by
the scribe David, and also by Archichippos, in
995. 100 years later the designs were brought to
Tsargrad (Constantinople) by the Bishop
Samuel. From the collection of the Tsarevich
John Grigorievich of Georgia.

Further calligraphy and illuminations from the
Gospels (called 'of Pizounda') of the 11th
century. Formerly in the Imperial Public
Library, St Petersburg. Originating from the
church at the fortress of Pizounda, Abkhazi.

PLATE 58.

11th–12th centuries (Georgia).

Church calendar (*Minéia*) for the months of July and August for the year 1049. From the Asian Museum of the Academy of Sciences at St Petersburg. No. 123, 4°. Parchment. This MS was once the property of the Georgian Monastery of Golgotha at Jerusalem.

Illustrations for the commentaries of St John dated 1038. This manuscript was written at the Georgian Monastery of St Savva at Jerusalem by order of our Father in God, George Djvareli, during the reign of the Emperor Michael of Byzantium, and in Georgia, of Bagrat Kouropalata. From the collection of the Tsarevich John Grigorievich of Georgia.

PLATE 59.

12th–13th centuries (Georgia).

Ornamentation from the Gospels formerly in the library of Professor D.I. Tchoubinoff, St Petersburg. 4°. Parchment. Also some calligraphy taken from a 12th-century prayer book. The Royal Library, Berlin.

Fragment of a 14th-century Gospel from the Roumianzeff Museum, Moscow. No. 830, 4°. Parchment.

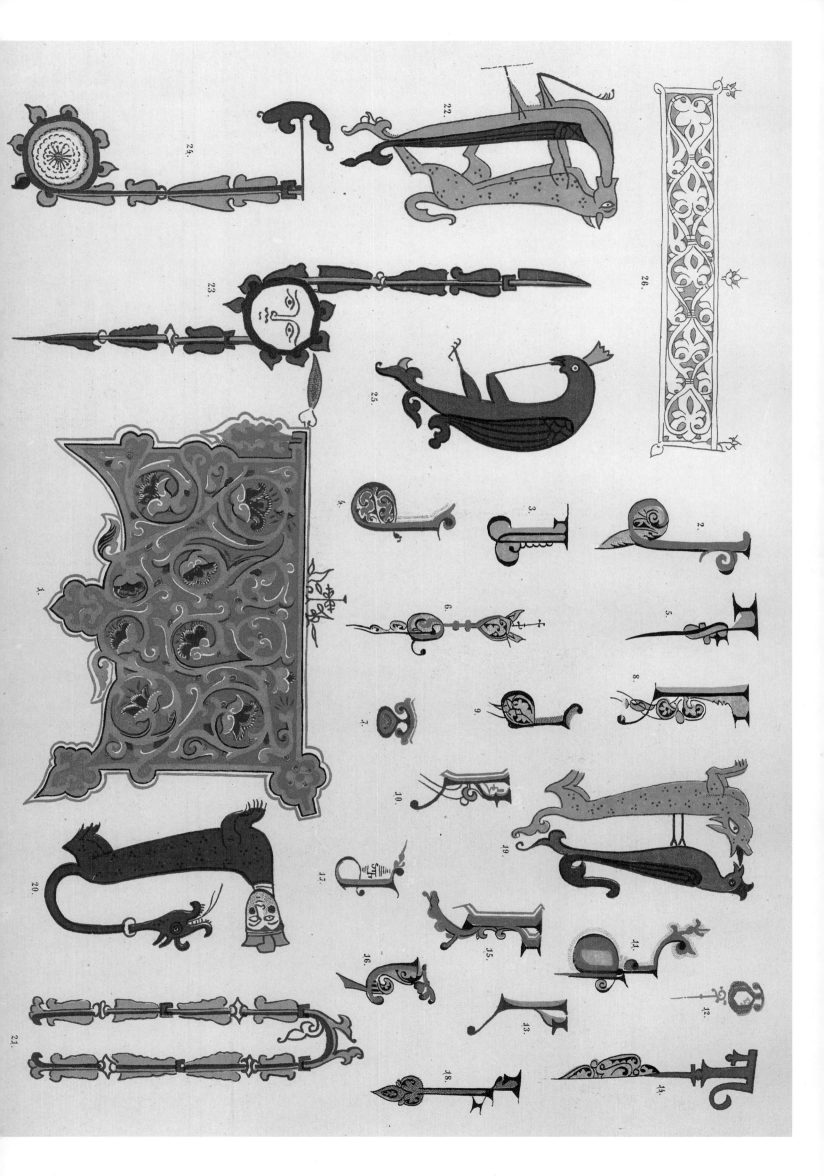

PLATE 60.

17th–18th centuries (Georgia).

From a 17th-century Book of Ritual in the Bibliotèque National de Paris, No. 1, 16°. Parchment. Note marginal illustrations and secular script.

Catachism and chronology from the years 1798–1816, in the library of Professor D.I. Tchoubinoff, St Petersburg, Very small format (85 mm in height). Written by Prince Soulkhan Orbiliani when he was either at Paris or Rome (where, for a while, he joined the Roman Catholic Church).

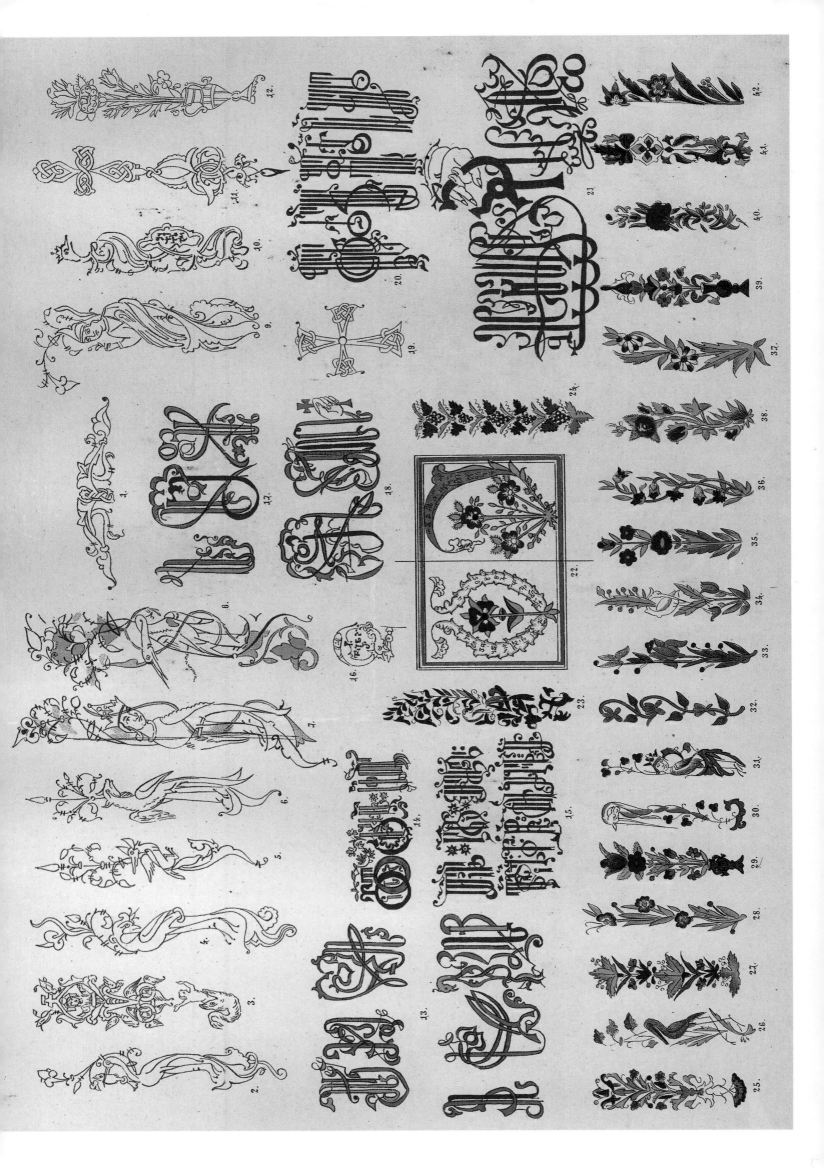

PLATE 61.
TEXTILES

A nineteenth century carpet consisting of numerous illustrated panels surrounding an embroidered coat of arms of the princely Gorchakoff family.

The Gorchakoffs were a noble Russian family of long standing and distinguished service to the State. Perhaps the best known member of this family was Russia's Chancellor, Prince Alexandre Mikhailovich Gorchakoff, during the reign of the Emperor Alexander II (1855–81).

PLATE 62.

EMBROIDERY

This embroidered purse or bag bears the
personal cypher of the last Romanov Emperor,
Nikolaie Alexandrovich.

PLATE 63.

EMBROIDERY

CEREMONIAL TOWELS

This towel has two identical terminals, one of which is shown here. It represents a Russian Tsar's symbols of office. The Cap of Monomakh is surmounted by the Orb, and a sword and sceptre of State are crossed beneath the Cap. The whole is decorated with ethnic, stylised designs.

PLATE 64.

CEREMONIAL TOWELS

This towel is designed with patriotic zeal. Its
somewhat naïve portrayal of a peasant woman's
life which surrounds the crowned cypher of the
Tsar Nikolai Alexandrovich, speaks of her
devotion to her Emperor. The whole is
surmounted by two crossed pre-revolutionary
flags. The workmanship is meticulous,
colourful and resounds with ethnic character,
even if it is of no particular quality.

PLATE 65.

APPLIQUÉ

Portrait after Franz Krüger of the Empress Alexandra Fedorovna, the Consort of Nicholas I, wearing a good example of a full *kokoshnik* together with its *fatta* (the veil).

Alexandra Fedorovna, born Princess Charlotte of Prussia, married Nicholas Pavlovich in 1817. The close dynastic ties between Russia and Prussia existed through most of the latter day Romanov rule.

PLATE 66.

A plate, cup and saucer from the Kremlin Service. Imperial Porcelain Factory. Nicholas I period.

A pair of porcelain salt containers that were made by Dmitri Vingradov for the Empress Elizabeth Petrovna. Imperial Porcelain Factory. 4 inches long, 1¼ inches high. These represent the earliest of Russian porcelain production, and are extremely rare.

An exceptionally fine plate in *bleu de Sèvres*, bearing the Imperial arms, the whole surrounded by military trophies and flower heads. Alexander III period.

A plate from the renowned Raphael Service, the decoration of which was taken from Catherine II's Logia at the Winter Palace (which, in its turn, had been copied from Raphael's Logia at the Vatican). Imperial Porcelain Factory, Alexander III period.

PLATE 67.

PORCELAIN

This series of plates was commissioned by Nicholas I from the Imperial Porcelain Factory in the early years of his reign. They proved so popular that they were produced in slightly varying forms during future reigns. It is of interest to note that in addition to the exquisite miniatures of the military subjects that were painted by the Imperial Porcelain Factory's greatest decorator artists (usually *after* paintings by K. Piratsky and V. Charlemagne), the plates' borders were decorated with particular artistry.

The three upper plates on our illustration consist of:

a. Soldiers of the Bashkir Division. This plate's border is decorated with a ribbon-tied laurel wreath which is surmounted by the Imperial Eagle. Alexander III period.

b. A mounted officer of the 2nd infantry Corps, and a gunner of the 2nd Mounted Artillery Brigade. The border is decorated with *ciselé* groups of swords and helmets which are interspersed by four Imperial Eagles with the dipped wings of the Nicholas I period.

c. Grenadiers of the Austrian Empire. The border is *en suite* to the preceiding one; the eagles, however, are Russian and not Austrian since they carry a miniature of the equestrian St George in their centres. This plate is dated 1835 on its back.

The four lower plates are of the Military Series' best quality. Their decoration consists of:

d. The two upper plates are of the Imperial Guards of the Preobrajhensky Regiment.

e. The two lower plates are of the 2nd Guard Cavalry Division, L.G. Dragoon Regiment.

All four plates carry *en plein* gold borders which are embellished with *ciselé* gilt groupings of swords and helmets entwined with decorative foliage, and the four flat-winged eagles that intersperse them are of the Nicholas I period.

All these plates are approximately 9 inches (24 cm) in diameter.

PLATE 68.

PORCELAIN

Three pieces from the Gardner Order Services.
l to *r*: A plate from the Order of Saint Alexandre
Nevsky. The ribbon of the Order encircles the
border, the star of the Order centres it.
9¼ inches (23.3 cm) diam.

Another from the Order of Saint Vladimir. The
ribbon and the star of the Order decorate it.
10⅜ inches.

A particularly rare plate from the Order of Saint
Andrew the Firstcalled, the highest Russian
Order of Chivalry. The collar of the Order
encirles the rim, the star of the Order centres it.
9¾ inches (24.7 cm) diam.

Three cups, saucers and covers from the era of
Catherine the Great. The ones to the left and
right of the illustration bear her cypher E II,
with the '2' painted through the central stroke
of the initial 'E' that stands for Ekaterina. This
cypher became the Imperial Porcelain Factory's
identification mark for the years during which
she reigned (1762–96). The central cup, saucer
and cover carry the Orlov cypher and arms.

PLATE 69.

PORCELAIN

One plate and two dishes from *The Kremlin Service.*

The Kremlin Service was commissioned by Nicholas I in 1836 from the Imperial Factory, the designs for which were executed by F.G. Solntzev. The motifs were inspired by 17th-century metalwork, a good deal of which was itself inspired by some Byzantine plates that were a part of Sophia Paleologue's dowry when she came to Russia as a bride for Ivan III.

The two large serving dishes measure 13¾ inches (35 cm) in diameter, and the dinner plate 12¾ inches (32.5 cm). The dishes are painted with stylised, undulating foliage with blue flowerheads, around a rust-coloured rosette on a black ground, surrounded by blue-green palmette motifs at intervals on burnished and matt-gilt grounds. The pattern, which is identical on the dinner plate, if in reduced dimension, is further enhanced with vari-coloured geometric and foliate motifs. There are other patterns that are incorporated into this vast service, but the ones which illustrate it are the most dramatic and delightful of them all. Each item is marked with the blue underglaze cypher of Nicholas I.

Two plates from the privately owned Youssoupov Factory that was founded by Prince Nikolai Borissovich Youssoupov in 1814.

The left-hand plate which is centred by two full-blown roses, the borders of which are painted with husk wreaths within gold bands, carries the inscription – *Rosier des Alpes* in gold. The second plate that is decorated with one rose and two buds carries the inscription – *La mousseuse de la flèche*, the borders being decorated *en suite* to the above. This service is known as *The Botanical Service* from the Archangelskoye Manufactory. 9½ inches (23.2 cm) diam.

PLATE 70.

PORCELAIN

Set of four porcelain plates made at the Imperial
Porcelain Factory for the Empress Elizabeth
Petrovna in *c.* 1750. Their relatively simple
pattern is, in fact, unique for no similar ones are
known to exist. The raised trellis decoration in
pale mauve and gold on a white ground is easily
recognisable and is sufficient to date them even
though the tiny underglazed black Imperial
eagles on their reverse identify the date of
production. 10¼ inches (26 cm) diam.

Part of a vast set of porcelain that was
commissioned by Catherine the Great for
Gregory Orlov. It is known as the Orlov
Service. Imperial Porcelain Factory, *c.* 1765.

The decoration consists of a *ciselé* gold
monogram, GGO (Graf – Count – Grigori
Orlov) within double gold bands, to either side
of which various scenes are painted – idyllic and
military scenes on a glazed white ground. The
borders are gold enriched with tiny blue dots.

A great deal has been written about this service
in view of its romantic connotations – not to
mention its quality which is superb. Gregory
Orlov was among the leading figures who
helped Catherine usurp the throne, and was one
of the brothers who assassinated her deposed
husband, Peter III, in 1762, a fact which haunted
her throughout her life. It is intriguing that no
mention is made of this service in Baron N.B.
de Wolff's monumental *History of the Imperial
Porcelain Factory* (1907). The service is said not
to have been 'discovered' until 1912.

162

PLATE 71.

PORCELAIN

Top Row
A porcelain Easter egg, first half of the 19th century, decorated with tooled gilding surrounding a picture of a bishop in Orthodox raiment. 4 inches high. A similar egg with a depiction of the Crucifixion. A particularly fine quality Easter egg with a delicately painted spray of flowers *en cartouche*.

Lower row
An Imperial presentation egg carrying the personal cypher of the Empress Alexandra Fedorovna surmounted by the cleft Russian Crown of State. Imperial Factory. An Imperial presentation egg carrying the personal cypher of the Empress Alexandra Fedorovna surmounted by the cleft Russian Crown of State. A small red cross on the reverse side indicates that the egg was made between the years 1914–17. The Empress usually presented such eggs at the *Tsarskaselskaya Obschchenna* – a small hospital at the palace where she worked as a nurse during the war years. Imperial Factory. Height 9cm (3½ inches).

PLATE 72.

PORCELAIN

A pair of magnificent vases bearing the portraits of Tsar Nicholas I and his Tsaritza, the Empress Alexandra Fedorovna. Imperial Porcelain Factory, dated 1836.

PLATE 73.

GLASS

Two cut glass wine glasses bearing the gold-crowned cypher of Alexander II (1855–1881) surrounded by battle standards, with a dramatic black eagle of State on the reverse side. Such glasses were usually created by the Imperial Glass Manufactory for use on the Imperial yachts. Height 19 cm (7½ inches).

PLATE 74.

GLASS

A cut glass carage and four matching goblets
from the Alexandrovsky Service. Imperial
Glasshouse Factory. 19th century.

Three examples from a glass service in use at
Livadia, in the Crimea. Designed by I. A.
Monigetti. 19th century.

PLATE 75.

ENAMELS

A pair of shaded enamel Easter eggs set on swirling silver-gilt stands by the Sazikov Brothers. Moscow, *c.* 1870. This was roughly the time when Fabergé began to design his magnificent *objet de vitrine* Easter eggs.

PLATE 76.

ENAMELS

A large silver *kovsh* decorated with lobed panels of scrolling vari-coloured foliage on a stippled gilt ground. By Ivan Saltykov, Moscow, 1899–1908.

This group consists of a circular *en plein* shaded silver/enamelled snuff box, the hinged lid depicting a young woman wearing a *kokoshnik* with a *fatta* (veil). By the 11th Artel, Moscow, 1908–17. 2¾ inches (7.2 cm) long. The tall, silver/enamel snuff box beside the preceding item is fashioned in a traditionally Russian medieval style. By Kurlioukov, 7¼ inches (18.5 cm) high. The other items are all prime examples of *cloisonné* enamelling.

L to *r*: a gold perfume flask in the form of a miniature samovar. 3½ inches (9 cm) high. A *Swiss* jewelled gold and *champlevé* enamel presentation snuff-box: Neufchatel, mid 19th century, maker's mark M.W.S. It was probably made to the order of the Emperor Alexander II, whose cypher in diamonds decorates the lid centred between four old mine-cut diamonds. This box is followed by a small gold and garnet-set box. St Petersburg, *c.* 1840, unidentified maker's mark W.G.

Although the art of the enameller was known in Kieven Rus and continued to be used for decorative purposes through the centuries, it was not until the accession of Catherine II ('the Great') in 1762 that there was a full appreciation for its beauty in Russia. Catherine collected enamels. She preferred the opaque white variety with the thin strips of bronze within which formed patterns. The nineteenth century saw its full flowering under the batons of such goldsmiths and jewellers as Ovchinnikov, Semonova, Morozov, Saltykov and Fabergé at which time the seven-toned, shaded variety was achieved.

PLATE 77.

ENAMELS

An important *guilloche* enamel silver-gilt table-clock. Marked Fabergé, workmaster Michael Pershin, St Petersburg, *c.* 1880, with inventory mark, N76743=.

An imaginative piece, this clock is of a square shape, decorated with translucent bright yellow enamel over a sunburst patterned *guilloché* ground which is applied with interlaced silver-gilt scrolls, some of which are set with rows of seed pearls. The circular while enamel dial carries black Roman numerals, surrounded by seed pearls set in a rose-gold mount and encircled by a chased silver-gilt *rocaille* frame, with a foliate and reeded outer border, ivory backing, and with Fabergé's customary silver scroll strut and case engraved in cyrillic.
4⅝ inches (11.7 cm) wide.

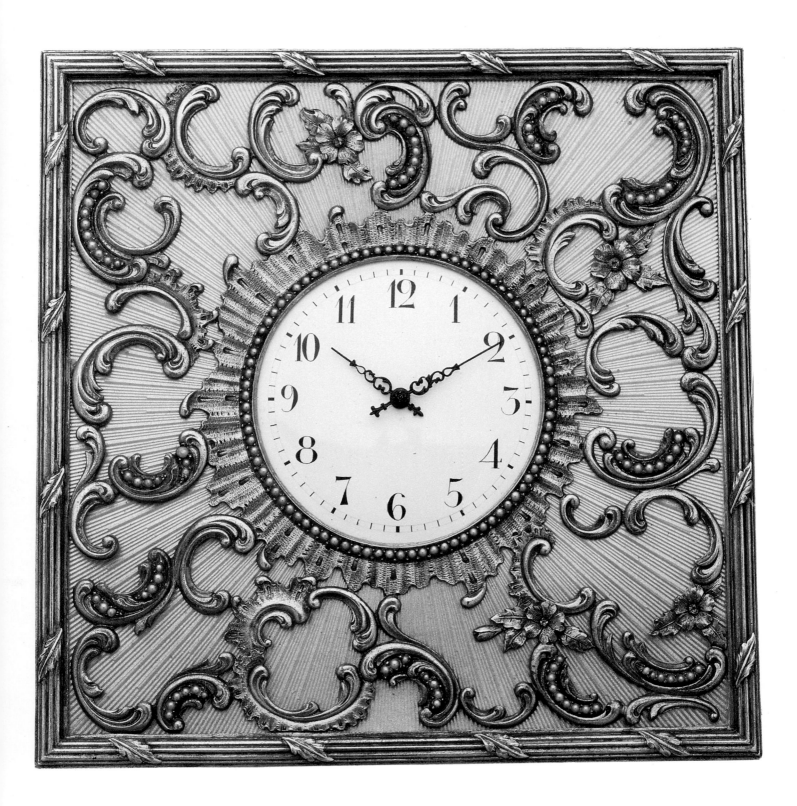

PLATE 78.

ENAMELS

A Fabergé *guilloche* enamel two colour
automaton Sedan Chair. The figure of a woman
is that of Catherine the Great who is borne by
two liveried blackamoors. Length 8.1 cm.

PLATE 79.

ENAMELS

All the Vitrine-piece Fabergé eggs were given names, this one is *The Pine Cone Egg*. The workmaster was Michael Pershin, St Petersburg, 1899–1900. 56 *zolotnik* standard (automaton key with post–1864 French import mark).

This egg is decorated with translucent blue enamel over a sunburst *guilloché* ground, encrusted with rose-cut diamond crescents, mounted in silver and gold, one end set with four petal-shaped portrait diamonds forming a quartrefoil enclosing the date 1900. The opposite end set with a rose-cut diamond star enclosing a cushion-shaped portrait diamond over a later miniature of a young woman. The egg opens to reveal (the surprise which Fabergé often incorporated into such eggs), in a fitted compartment, an oxidised silver elephant automaton with ivory tusks, supporting an enamelled mahout seated upon a gold-fringed *guilloché* saddle-cloth, each side set with three rose-cut diamond collets, one covering a key-hole. When wound with the original gold key, the elephant lumbers forward, swaying its head and swishing its tail. Height of egg: 9.5 cm; length of elephant: 5 cm.

Carl Fabergé, jeweller and goldsmith to the Russian Imperial Court, delivered approximately 56 Easter eggs between the years 1885 and 1916. The whereabouts of only 46 are known.

PLATE 80.

ENAMELS

A silver and enamel Imperial presentation portfolio. The inscriptions read: *To Their Imperial Majesties the Sovereign Emperor Nicholas Alexandrovich and the Sovereign Empress Alexandra Feodorovna. From the City Society of Ivanovo-Voznesensky, November 14, 1894.*

This rectangular burgundy velvet portfolio is mounted with a chased silver plaque applied with a diamond-set cypher N.A., for Nicholas and Alexandra within the chased Imperial mantle that is decorated with red enamel and inscribed, *God be With Us* above a stylised two-headed eagle. The centre and base are inscribed with dedication inscriptions in blue enamel with applied scroll and eagle spandrels. The whole has a *cloisonné* enamel floral and beaded border. Overall size – 16½ × 12¼ inches (42 × 31 cm).

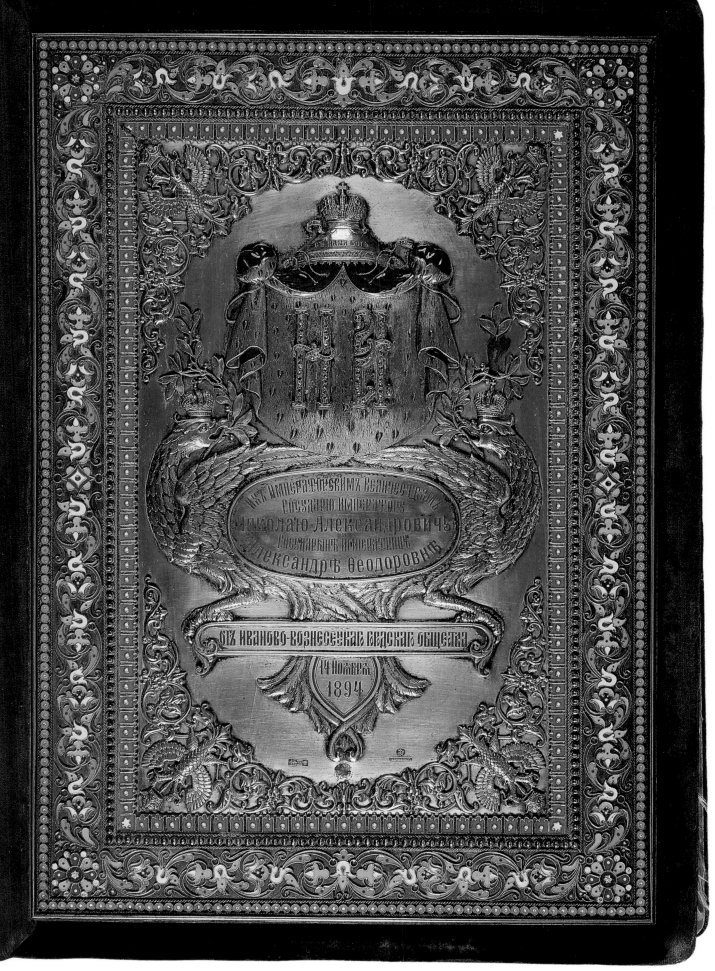

PLATE 81.

METALWORK

Gold bracelet decorated with a frieze of fabulous
beasts. Sarmatian, 2nd century B.C.
1¾ — 2½ inches.

The Sarmatians were a tribe from eastern
Europe. They appear in the early fourth century
B.C., and together with the Scythian
Ploughmen, were among the more important
peoples to form the nucleus of the Russian
Slavonic race.

The Sarmatians were great horsemen and
hunters as the decoration of this bracelet would
suggest. Originally nomadic, they finally
settled down to an agricultural stability, and,
although they are not considered to have been as
sophisticated as the Scythians, their
contribution to early Russian history was of
considerable importance. Both races were well
known to the Greeks and Romans.

PLATE 82.

METALWORK

A traditional presentation *kovsh* from the reign of Elisabeth Petrovna (1741–62). Silver gilt, with unrecorded workmaster's initials, G.I., Moscow, 1751. It is decorated with a large Imperial eagle of State which indicates that it was an Imperial gift.

A pair of similar *kovshi* to the one above, but of a more ornate nature for they carry the eagle of State on their bows. They also carry presentation inscriptions on their sides as was the custom. They are unmarked other than their date of production – 1750.

PLATE 83.

METALWORK

A fine example of Russian *niello* work. This silver-gilt and delicately nielloed beaker of tapering cylindrical form depicts a female figure on a fish scale ground within an oval upon the edges of which rest two nymphs. Further designs decorate the whole which stands 16.5 cm in height. It bears no hallmark other than the word Moscow signifying its area of production.

PLATE 84.

METALWORK

An important silver-gilt centrepiece forming a
fruit stand and six branch candelabrum. From
the Sazikov Factory with pre-revolutionary
Russian hallmarks. St Petersburg, 1849.
Height: 31⅞ inches.

PLATE 85.

JEWELLERY

This collection of East European jewellery is not all of Russian origin, some of the pieces are Hellenistic. The earrings (No. 1), and the bracelet (No. 2), however, are of unquestionable provenance.

1. This matching pair of earrings are Southern Russian and of the 4th century B.C. Each comprises an elaborate disc with filigree and granulation, the centre of the rosette retaining traces of enamel. From the rosettes festoons of gold braids, pendant tassels of loop-in-loop chain, gold beads and gold coloured glass pendants. The festoons and rosettes probably linked in modern times.

2. South Russian gold and garnet beaded cruciform elements threaded between gold disc beads into a bracelet. 13½ inches long (34.3 cm), diamond roundels. 4th century B.C.

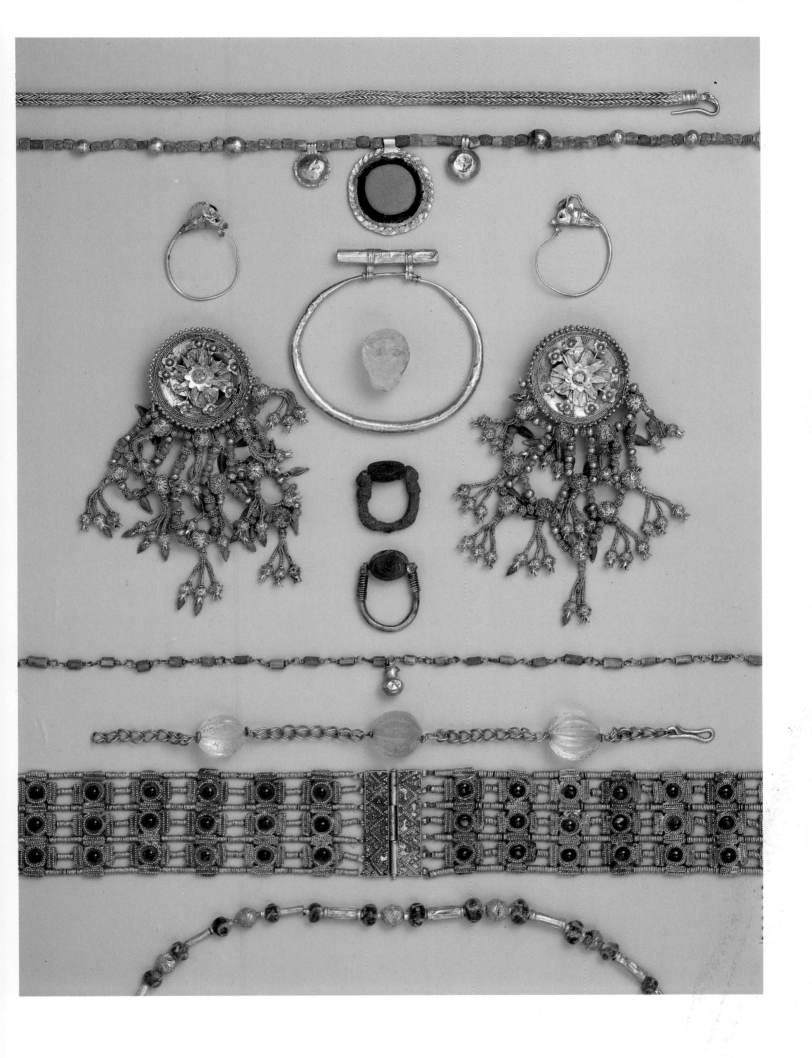

PLATE 86.

JEWELLERY

Two ropes of Russian *brelki*, or miniature Easter eggs, and a few loose ones. Some of these eggs are by the firm of Fabergé. Second half of the 19th century.

PLATE 87.

ICONS

Icon of the Virgin of Vladimir. Moscow School
c. 1500, 31.5 × 26 cm.

The original version of this particular
representation of the Holy Mother and her
Child is of Byzantine origin. It was brought to
Russia in the 12th century where its initial place
of rest was a monastery near Kiev. It was
removed by Andrei Bogolioubsky to his own
capital city, Vladimir, when he conquered Kiev
in 1169. It was housed in the Cathedral of the
Virgin's Dormition (Assumption). On the fall
of the Vladimir-Suzdalian principality to the
Tartars, the icon was removed yet again, this
time to Moscow where it was lodged in the
Uspensky Cathedral. Today, in remarkably fine
condition, the Vladimir Virgin hangs at the
Tretiakov Gallery in Moscow. It is considered
by the authorities to be one of the country's
greatest treasures. The people, however, look
upon it as *Russia's Pallium.*

This is an icon of *Oumilenie* (Tenderness), and
the Child is always shown seated on His
Mother's right arm, with His arm round her
neck and with the sole of His left foot showing.
Her left hand points towards Him in the manner
of a stern *Hodigitria* icon.

PLATE 88.

ICONS

A *Jitye*, or Lifecycle, icon of the Prophet Elijah. The small depictions which surround the central painting of the prophet's ascent in the Fiery Chariot are the biblical stories of his life and miracles. The surrounding *basma* carries an inscription naming the icon, as well as an additional Saint. This Saint is probably a 'family Saint', that of the individual for whom the icon was originally commissioned. *c.* 1600.

PLATE 89.
ICONS

An icon of the Archangel Michael, the *Archistrategos*, whose wings denote that he is the Messenger of God. He carries the sword with which he defends the Church, sometimes this is replaced by a trident. This was painted by an unknown artist of the Stroganov School of Iconography in about 1600.

PLATE 90.

ICONS

Christ Enthroned – The Pantocrator
16th century. Moscow. 68.5 × 54 cm.

The Saviour is presented seated on His throne with His right hand raised in blessing, His left hand holds an open book which bears the text: *Come, blessed of my Father, for whom the Kingdom has been prepared.* He is surrounded by a double mandorla within which angels swirl, indicating the presence of divine cosmic powers. At the four corners of a curved rectangle the Four Evangelists are represented by their symbols – a bull for Luke, an angel for Matthew, an eagle for Jonh, and a lion for Mark – indicating that the Saviour's Word has reached the four corners of the world.

All manner of interpretations can be attributed to this icon – the subject is described in Revelations 4 verses 2–3 and 6–9. In Russia the first painting of Christ so presented is considered to have been by a Greek iconographer, Theophanese, or Feophan Grek, as the Russians called him. His 14th century panel is now in the Cathedral of the Annunciation at the Moscow Kremlin.

PLATE 91.

ICONS

A pair of Tsar Gates (being Russian they are not 'Royal Doors'), with the Annunciation depicted on the two upper registers, and SS. Matthew and John below. This is not traditional: the Four Evangelists should be depicted upon four lower registers. These icons are of excellent quality, probably Moscow, and from the 16th century.

PLATE 92.

ICONS

A late 17th-century triptych of St Nicholas the Wonder-worker whose icon is flanked by two Saints in attendance, the whole is surmounted by the non-canonical *New Testament Trinity* representations of which are condemned by the fundamentalist Church (since no-one has seen God the Father He cannot be depicted). The decoration of this triptych is typical of the seventeenth century.

PLATE 93.

A COLLECTION OF RUSSIAN ICONS IN SILVER *RIZAS*

Icons presented in the traditional silver *rizas* for keeping in the home, usually in the 'Red Corner' of a bedroom. A *lampada*-lamp would burn a perpetual light suspended before them.

The collection represents many subjects of the Orthodox Christian faith. 17th–19th centuries.

PLATE 94.

ICONS

An 18th-century icon of St Nicholas the
Wonder-worker painted in an earlier tradition.
The *basma* and *oklad* (the surround and overlay)
are of silver fashioned by Afanasii and Stepan
Popov at Veliki Ustioug, between the years
1761–76. 59 × 48.5 cm.

PLATE 95.

ICONS

A folding triptych of *The Neroukatvorny Spas* (*the 'Not Made with Hands'*, or, *the 'Veronica'*). Christ is flanked by a Saint and an incorrectly placed Angel who is turned away from Him. This icon is of two-coloured gold and enamelled. It is by Erik Kollin, a Fabergé workmaster. It is marked St Petersburg and dated 1888. Height, 4 inches.

PLATE 96.

PAPIER MÂCHÉ

A Hexagonal Papier Mâché Box, *c.* 1860.
The lid is painted with a general view of the
Moscow Kremlin. The sides are painted with
the various towers of the Kremlin's walls
including the Gateway of the Saviour, the
St Nicholas, the Holy Trinity and the Tsar's
towers. This box is unusual in that its
background is white and not the more
traditional black. Height 3½ inches, the width,
5½ inches.

PLATE 97.

PAPIER MÂCHÉ

Two well-painted papier mâché Easter eggs.
The red egg is painted with a version of *The
Descent into Hell*: Christ has broken the gates of
Hell which now form a cross at His feet, and
angels are helping sinners to come out from the
abyss. The blue egg carries a depiction of
St Xenia. Height 5½ inches (14 cm).

Neither egg is marked but more likely than not
they both came from either the Lukoutin or
Vishniakov Factories, certainly not from the
workshops of Palekh where papier mâché work
only began after 1917.

PLATE 98.

A particularly fine box by the Vishniakov
Factory, third quarter of the 19th century, of a
summer troika (a cart) against a vivid blue sky.
Width 9¼ inches.

A box by the Vishniakov Factory bearing a
depiction of a winter troika. Width 11 inches.

A box by the Lukoutin Factory, the lid painted
with a romantic moonlit scene of figures in a
boat near a leafy shore. Height 4½ inches.

A tea caddy by the Vishniakov Factory. 19th
century, shows a dashing summer troika.
3½ inches.

A lacquered wooden box by the Vishniakov
Factory, dated 1875. The lid is painted with a
finely detailed view of the Moscow Kremlin.
4 inches.

A single Easter egg in two sections, the first
depicting Christ's Resurrection, the second,
St Alexis, Metropolitan of Russia. An
interesting inscription indicates that this egg
was produced by the Moscow Association of
Old Believers at the Transfiguration
Bogodelnetsky ('good works') House. Metal
suspension ring. Height 6½ inches.

PLATE 99.

KARELIAN BIRCH FURNITURE

A fine example of Russian Karelian-birch furniture representing the standard of workmanship achieved in Russia, and the use of the wood described in the General Introduction.

A bow-fronted and brass-mounted side cabinet, the stepped top fitted with a drawer above two doors simulating eight drawers with three graduated drawers below. The fluted angles are headed by roundels, the sides panelled, on square tapering feet. Width 33 inches (84 cm); height 65 inches (165 cm) 17 inches (43 cm) deep. Early 19th century.

PLATE 100.

MALACHITE

An ormolu-mounted malachite table with a circular top with beaded border, mounted on a baluster shaft applied with strapwork clasps and a band of berried foliage. The whole supported by four grotesque beasts with wings. The perfectly assembled malachite pieces which form the veneer are of the *Miatoi Barkhot* ('crushed velvet') variety.

19th century. Height 31 inches (78.5 cm): diameter 27 inches (70 cm).

The central amphora-shaped urn is decorated with fire-gilt ormolu in a traditional manner. Its interest lies in the impressively faultless manner in which the malachite chip veneer has been worked to form the perfect pattern on a rounded surface.

The pair of side vases are of superb quality, fire-gilt and campana-shaped. They are decorated with a frieze of bacchantes below a band of vine, the handles rising from a pair of masks worked with scrolling acanthus. The malachite bases on which they are mounted are of the *Miatoi Barkhot* pattern.

Mid 19th century. Height 19¾ inches (49.8 cm).